ENTREPRENEURIAL D

PEG SERIES
(Practical Exercises for Groups)
General Series Editor: Humphrey Shaw

The PEG Series is designed to improve managers' (and trainee managers')
analytical and problem solving, decision making and presentational
skills. Most titles in the Series include compuer disk simulations
for group use, case studies and supporting Trainer's Manuals which contain
model answers, notes, transparencies, and other training support material.

Decision Making, the first in the Series, comprises:
This book of case studies

plus, accompanying

Trainer's Manual

Suggested model answers to the case studies, overhead projection
transparencies and other supporting material. isbn 0 946139 47 4 £49.99

also

House Building Management Simulation
Trainer's Manual and computer simulation for group training on
the management of property development. isbn 0 946139 19 9 £99.99
(educational edition isbn 0 946139 29 6 £49.99)

Football Management Simulation
Trainer's Manual and computer simulation for group training
based on football team management. isbn 0 946139 09 1 £99.99
(educational edition isbn 0 946139 24 5 £49.99)

Restaurant Management Simulation
trainer's Manual and computer simulation for group training
on the running of a restaurant. isbn 0 946139 14 8 £99.99
(educational edition isbn 0 946139 34 2 £49.99)

All software is priced without VAT which must be added.

Entrepreneurial Decision making

Humphrey Shaw

Brian Dakin   Jon Carter   Wayne Griffiths

PEG SERIES

This first edition of Entrepreneurial Decision Making is published by ELM Publications of 12 Blackstone Road, Huntingdon PE18 6EF (0480-414553) on April 30th, 1990.

Printed in Great Britain by St Edmundsbury Press, Bury St Edmunds, Suffolk.

isbn 0 946139 69 5

PEG Series No. MC2

To our parents

CONTENTS

Introduction

Case Studies	Topic	Page

INDIVIDUAL ENTERPRISE DECISIONS

THE BUSINESS ENVIRONMENT & ENTERPRISE DECISIONS

ORGANISATIONAL ENTERPRISE DECISIONS

MARKETING ENTERPRISE DECISIONS

FINANCIAL ENTERPRISE DECISIONS

INTRODUCTION

Ever since governments took responsibility for the level of economic activity within the economy, they have been trying to encourage entrepreneurial activity. In the 1960's and 1970's the trend was towards what can best be described as collective corporate enterprise, where Government Ministers used to sit down with the representatives of industry and trade union leaders and discuss how the three parties could bring about economic enterprise. During the last ten years the Government has preferred to leave economic planning to market forces and entrepreneurial decision making. Whichever system is favoured by governments in a market economy, all firms owe their existence to an entrepreneur who is able to market a product or service which the market wants, and at a price which allows the entrepreneur to make a profit.

Entrepreneurial enterprise, therefore, is not new but it is only recently that business schools have included it as a subject in undergraduate and postgraduate courses. The purpose of this book of case studies is to show prospective business students all the areas which they must consider before starting a new venture. It covers the raising of capital and deciding what form of business to start up; the consideration of economic factors which affect business; and the entrepreneurial skills needed to manage the new enterprise and market its product or service, while maintaining financial control.

Many new businesses fail not because of poor entrepreneurial ideas but because the entrepreneurs lacked the necessary skills to manage a growing business. This book will be useful to both students and people considering setting up a new business on their own for the first time.

I would like to thank the following people for their many useful suggestions and comments:- Geoff Bath MSc (Hatfield Polytechnic), Rita Crompton BA (Luton College of H.E.), James

Hogg MSc (Watford College), Helena Shaw BA PhD (Dacorum College), Sally Messenger MSc (University of Surrey), Andy Faed (Investment Manager, City Bank), Derek Belcher (Director, University Packing), Robert Weeks (Director, Court Farm) and Sue Badger (Characters Desk Top Publishing). Lastly I would like to thank Sheila Ritchie and all the staff at Elm Publications for their help with the production of the P.E.G. series.

Humphrey Shaw

MR AND MRS SCOTT

Mr. and Mrs. Scott have been married for twelve years. They live in a semi detached house in Surbiton. Since buying the house they have seen it appreciate considerably in value and they believe that it is now worth £160,000. Their £10,000 mortgage on the property is now very small by present day standards and the Scotts have building society savings of £17,000.

Last year Mr. Scott celebrated his fortieth birthday and since then he has been suffering from the usual mid life blues. His wife is similarly unhappy with her job and they would like to purchase a sub Post Office in the country and run a local village store.

With this aim in mind they have been searching the pages of the classified advertisements and have found a sub Post Office for sale in a village near Chard in Somerset. The Scott's are considering selling their house and investing their life savings in the new venture. They would have to give up their jobs and their combined salary of £24,000 per annum.

Last month they approached their local bank manager to ask her opinion. She told them that nowadays many couples are starting their own businesses and that there is less risk attached to purchasing an existing business than from starting a completely new venture. The bank manager believes that the project could prove to be a great success but ends the conversation with the following words of advice. "My last boss always used to say, "Never forget the opportunity costs of starting a business."

Mr and Mrs Scott did not like to say that they did not understand what opportunity costs are and have asked you the following questions?

1 What are opportunity costs?

2 What are the Scott's opportunity costs?

3 Why do accountants not take opportunity costs into consideration when calculating a firm's profit and loss?

4 Why is it important for the Scott's to consider the opportunity costs of buying a sub Post Offfice and village store?

MARKET DAY AT DORCHESTER

Dorchester is an attractive town situated on the south coast of England. The town is surrounded by attractive countryside and has a very good shopping centre. Once a week in a car park on the outskirts of the town there is a local market. Market traders come to sell their wares which range from local vegetable produce to household goods and clothes.

Some of the traders have been coming to this market for many years and have stands which stock a large range of merchandise. Others are very small and have been started by new entrepreneurs who are hoping to expand their businesses in the near future.

All of the traders know that if their business is to prosper they must provide goods which their customers want. The traders have to take account of changes in consumers' tastes, incomes and preferences. As a result the type of merchandise which is offered for sale in the market is constantly changing. Those traders which do not offer products which the market want soon find that their sales and profits are low. If sales do not improve they eventually leave because they cannot earn a normal profit. When this happens the traders will either seek a different market, or start another business, or seek paid employment.

1 How does the market economy allocate goods and services in an economy?

2 In what way is a local market representative of the market economy?

3 What is meant by the term normal profit?

4 Why is it important for the traders at Dorchester Market to earn a normal profit?

WHITE GATE FARM

White Gate Farm is a 400 acre farm situated in the attractive Gloucestershire countryside. It is owned and managed by John and Teresa King. John inherited the farm from his parents in 1973 just as Britain joined the European Community.

John and Teresa King had wanted Britain to join the European Community because they believed that the Common Agricultural Policy would help British Farmers. John had attended many rallies held by the Farmer's Union and had spoken at several fund raising dinners in favour of joining the EC.

The first few years following Britain's entry were indeed good. The farm continued to invest heavily in new labour-saving devices. New tractors and a combine harvester were bought and an additional £100,000 was invested in new barns, and milking sheds. By 1980 the farm only employed two full time people and relied on local casual workers during the busy harvest time.

John and Teresa King also found it relatively easy to borrow during this period. Interest rates were low in real terms after allowing for inflation and farm land was increasing steadily in price. However, the King family were still cautious and resisted the offer of further loans from the bank manager for additional improvements. The slump of the 1930s had had a strong influence on his father and that caution had been passed down to the son. John's father had used to talk of the idle acres when it was sometimes even uneconomic to harvest the crops and when land prices fell sharply. As a result John's father had become a survivor, only making small investments, and conserving the farm's resources in case the slump returned. This had meant that over the years the farm had become uncompetitive but the substantial investment in the 1970s meant that the farm was once again competitive.

The early 1980s were again tough for farmers. High interest rates coupled with increased oil and fertiliser costs meant that profits were again squeezed. The farm had always been mixed with about half the farm given over to grazing and the balance to growing wheat and barley. Many farms in the area had begun to specialise but John felt that if times were hard one could always feed the cattle and survive on the milk cheque. The milk cheques also helped to ease cash flow problems as once the winter wheat was planted no money could be gained from it until the following summer. The seed and fertiliser had to be bought on overdraft and high interest rates reduced profit margins.

From 1980 to 1985 the farm again seemed to be just surviving. Milk quotas and expensive fertilisers meant that John was reluctant to invest additional capital in the farm. The high interest rates had also reduced profit margins and the farm was beginning to look in need of more investment to see it into the 1990s.

During John's working life he had seen the end of the small farmer. The 100 acre farm was no longer economic and John feared that the same situation would force his son Lawrence who was now 16 to consider another occupation. Lawrence had worked with his father from an early age and was keen to continue the family tradition of farming. His ancestors had farmed the Gloucestershire countryside for several generations. A photograph of Lawrence's Great Grandfather sitting on an early steam tractor was still hanging in the hall. The picture, apart from having sentimental value, reinforced the need for investing for the tractor had allowed the farm to make savings in labour thereby making it one of the most modern farms at the turn of the century.

The family decided that they would try to purchase another farm of the same size so long as it was convenient to their present one. If this was not possible they would sell their present farm and buy a larger farm in the county. John instructed the local estate agent to keep him informed of any future farm sales and made arrangements with the local bank manager to raise the necessary money to finance the venture.

For the next two years interest rates continued to fall and profits in the industry continued to rise. In late 1988 inflationary pressures began to worry the government and interest rates started to rise. This increase in rates continued into 1989 but in May of that year a 400 acre farm was put on the market by its owners who had decided to retire as their children had chosen other careers. After lengthy negotiations the King family acquired the farm making it the largest investment decision which the family had ever made.

1 What factors influenced the King's investment decision?

2 Why were the Kings still prepared to invest inspite of an increase in interest rates?

3 Why is investment important in an economy?

4 Why was John King's father so reluctant to invest in the farm?

WHEATSHEAF FOODS

Wheatsheaf foods was founded in 1979 by Christopher Marshall and Robin Jones. They had both studied food science at university and had become concerned about the increasing use of chemical fertilisers and additives in food. Their aim was to form a food company which would manufacture specialist foods for health shops.

When Christopher and Robin started their company they could just afford the £100 initial share capital and the cost of registering the company at Companies' House. As a result their first product had to be made in Robin's parents' kitchen. Their first product was a range of biscuits which were produced using stone ground flour. The biscuits contained no artificial additives or preservatives and were sold in the local market.

After three months trading the firm gained valuable publicity by being featured in the local newspaper. Local consumers liked the firm's products and sales of the biscuits began to grow. It was at this point that Christopher's uncle Henry decided to support their business venture. He agreed to buy 10 per cent of Christopher's shares in the firm for £10,000. This gave the Wheatsheaf sufficient funds to rent a small industrial unit in the town and to invest in the latest ovens and other catering equipment which they needed.

During the next two years the firm started to employ additional staff and was able to sell its products to local health food outlets. The firm launched a range of other products from mueslis to cakes and after five years of trading Wheatsheaf foods had become an employer of over 100 people with sales approaching £1 million a year.

By the middle 1980s the firm was enjoying buoyant trading conditions. Consumers were becoming increasingly health conscious and the firm was beginning to get its products stocked in some of the smaller supermarket chains. This had lead to rapid sales growth but had left the company with a heavy debt burden. At the end of 1987 Wheatsheaf foods owed its bankers £4.5 million and the firm owed another £2 million to creditors.

These were not the only problems. The two directors no longer made all of the management decisions themselves. As the firm had grown three new directors had been appointed and a management structure had been installed after the appointment of a firm of managment consultants. This had lead to complaints from the work force about changes in working practices and conditions. Many of the older work force felt that the company had lost its friendly atmosphere. About 60% of the work force had joined the Transport and General Workers Union and although the firm had agreed to union recognition there was a feeling amongst some of the management that strikes and other industrial action could become the way of the future.

Christopher and Robin were becoming increasingly unhappy about the future direction of their company. Their bank manager advised them to seek a listing on the Unlisted Securities Market. This policy he assured them would allow the company to pay off its debts, have sufficient funds for new investment and would make Christopher and Robin millionares overnight.

In 1988 when the firm had its annual holiday the three shareholding directors Christopher, Robin and Henry decided to take a week-end break to discuss the future. They decided to go to the small Welsh town of Dolgellau where they could walk in the beautiful countryside and discuss what future action they should take.

8

As the three directors drove back to their homes on Sunday night they agreed that they would put their plan to the work force. The firm would not seek a listing on the Unlisted Securities market but would instead take steps to become a co-operative. The company would still have a Board of Directors but it would have to report to the workforce each year, and all workers would receive a dividend so long as the firm continued to make a profit. The workers would be asked to purchase shares in the co-operative and if they agreed this would partly reduce the company's debts. The rest of the money would be raised by selling the freehold of the unit and negotiating with an insurance company to lease it back. All workers would have one vote, and worker committes would be set up to discuss such matters as pay rises, working conditions, new product development and recruitment policies.

When the workers arrived back from their annual holiday they saw notices displayed asking them to attend an important company meeting on Saturday evening in the local town hall. Rumours immediately began to spread throughout the factory but the directors wished to keep their plans secret. Many workers who knew that the firm was in debt feared redundancy or a merger with a larger food company.

At the meeting Robin outlined his idea of forming a co- operative. He explained to the workers how it would work and handed them a draft constitution for them to consider. There would be no pressure on anyone to purchase shares, and all workers would receive between 100 and 1000 shares depending upon their length of time with the company. The new shares would cost £5 each and would carry a dividend which would be decided by the co-operative once the firm had finalised its annual accounts. In the first instance the company would be issuing one million new shares, and next month there would be a further meeting at the town hall for the work force to ask questions. After that there would be a vote to decide whether or not the firm should become a co-operative with every employee being allowed one vote. A simple majority would decide the issue.

In December the firm held its election. The vote would be carried out by the Electoral Reform Society and the result would be made known in January. Every worker was given a voting form and a pre-paid envelope and was aked to send their vote to the Society. When the votes were counted 88% of the work force had voted and there was overwhelming support for turning the firm into a co-operative. In January the directors announced the result and told the work force that the firm's solicitors were being instructed to draw up the necessary documents. In the meantime the firm would continue with its existing organisational structure until the co-operative could come into being at the end of the year.

1 Why do you think the directors decided to form a co-operative?

2 What are the benefits of co-operatives compared with other forms of business entities?

3 Are co-operatives compatable with the government's aim to encourage an enterprise culture?

BYGONE INDUSTRIES

For years David Baldwin had enjoyed collecting postcards. Over the years he had built up a large collection by regularly attending post card fairs and auctions. His main interest has been street scenes but over the years he has also collected other cards such as advertising and railway postcards.

This year his employer offered him the chance to take early retirement. David is 55 and the employer agreed to pay him his pension immediately and to give him a lump sum of £25,000. David is fortunate in that he no longer has a mortgage and would like to use the money to start a small antique shop specialising in old postcards.

David is concerned about the legalities of working for himself. He does not know whether he should form a limited company or whether he should operate as a sole trader or form a partnership. David has been advised to discuss the matter at his local Citizens Advice Bureau. You work there advising clients on business matters and have been asked the following questions.

1 What do I need to do before I can start trading?

2 What are the advantages/disadvantages of being a sole trader?

3 What are the advantages/disadvantages of forming a partnership?

4 What are the advantages/disadvantages of forming a company?

VANN INDUSTRIES

Vann industries was formed five years ago by Hugh and Lorraine Vann. They were both keen campers and they believed that they could make a better small tent than was currently on the market.

Their aim was to manufacture a light weight tent which could sleep two people and which could be folded into a small bag which could be easily carried by campers. Their revolutionary design proved to be very successful. The firm received good publicity from the camping magazines and some of this coverage reached the Italian media. Orders started to flow in from Italian camping shops and soon the firm was selling ten per cent of its sales in the Italian market. Inspired by their success Vann Industries appointed consultants in Germany and France to secure exclusive distribution rights with certain camping shops. As a result the firm now exports a third of its production.

Last week Lorraine saw an advertisement in the national papers inviting companies to apply for a Queens Award for Export if they believed that their achievements merited such an award. She would like to apply but would like to know more about the award and has asked you the following questions.

1 What is the Queens Award for Export and who may apply?

2 Why does the government promote such a scheme?

3 What proportion of exports are accounted for by small companies?

4 What effect will the single European market have on firms like Vann industries?

THE HEALTH CENTRE

For the last ten years Dr Khan has worked as a partner in a surgery in the North of England. The practice has been run from the downstairs of a large Edwardian house with the senior partner living in the upstairs. The senior partner has now decided to retire and has agreed to sell the house to Dr Khan.

Dr Khan already has a house in Manchester where he lives with his wife and two children. He would like to be able to use some of his savings and borrow the balance of the money to purchase the senior partner's house. Dr khan would then like to refurbish the house and employ a nurse and three other doctors. His aim is to offer local patients twenty-four hour a day medical cover under the National Health. Patients would not need to book an appointment but would simply arrive and be able to see a doctor. Each doctor would work certain set times so that patients could be certain of seeing the same doctor.

The local health authority and the planning department have approved the scheme. Dr Khan now needs to raise the necessary finance and to promote his plan.

You are one of Dr Khan's patients and you work as a free lance Business Consultant. He has asked you to advise him and has asked you the following questions.

1 How can I raise the money for the new venture?

2 What information will the lenders require?

3 How should I repay the loan?

4 What are the risks involved in borrowing money to finance business expansion?

PLASTIC MOULDINGS

Plastic Mouldings is a large plc whose core business is manufacturing injection moulding machines which are used by a host of companies in the United Kingdom and around the world. As well as manufacturing molding machines the firm also has a number of other businesses which have been acquired as a result of mergers and takeovers during the last twenty years.

The Board of directors have just completed their five year plan and have decided to dispose of the plastic toy division which specialises in manufacturing children's dolls, farm animals, sports equipment and other children's toys. This part of the firm has faced increasing competition from imports and the firm has seen its return on capital employed in this division drop from 12% in 1983 to 8% in 1989. The business has been valued at £7 million and Plastic Mouldings would now like to sell it.

The toy division's managing director is Barbara Jenkins who has worked hard with her other directors and fifty production workers to ensure that the firm's factory in a depressed northern town remains a profitable and viable business. As a result she and her other co-directors are reluctant to see the firm sold to a competitor who would probably manufacture the firm's successful products overseas and turn the operation into just another merchandising concern with the loss of most of the jobs at the factory.

Barbara and the other directors are convinced that they can generate a greater return on capital employed than is presently being earned. The directors have approached the main board of directors to ask if they can purchase the company as a management buy out with the aim of later seeking a listing on the Unlisted Securities Market.

The directors of Injection Moulding have agreed providing the firm can raise the necessary finance and have given Barbara three months in which to complete the buy out.

1 What is a management buy out?

2 Why do you think Barbara and her other directors are prepared to take the risks of a management buy out?

3 How can the directors raise the money for the buy out?

4 What factors will Injection Moulding have taken into account in valuing the toy division at £7 million?

THE SANDWICH BAR

Janet and Margaret had always wanted to run their own business and in 1990 the two women decided to leave their clerical jobs in a large insurance firm and set up their sandwich bar in a small shop near their former employer.

The two women were able to put £30,000 into the business and their local bank manager agreed to lend them an additional £25,000. This meant that they were able to acquire the lease on the shop which they wanted and purchase the necessary cooking equipment to start the business.

The previous year had seen a lot of cases of food poisoning and both Janet and Margaret were determined that their sandwich bar would meet the highest levels of hygiene. All of their food had a short shelf life and the directors decided that in the first instance they would purchase most of their food in bulk from local supermarkets as they lacked the necessary turnover to deal with the large food wholesalers. Inevitably the firm's prices were a little higher than some of their competitors but Janet and Margaret believed that customers in that area were prepared to pay for a premium product.

The firm has just completed its first six months of trading and has made a small profit. Janet and Margaret are pleased and have decided to recruit two extra staff to help them in the kitchen. During the first six months of trading both women have earned less than they did with their former employer and they have also had to work longer hours. However, both are agreed that it was the correct thing for them to do and believe that in the future they will be able to increase their earnings.

1 Why do you think Janet and Margaret wanted to set up their own business?

2 In what way has their decision benefitted the United Kingdom's economy?

3 Why is it important that their business makes a profit after Janet and Margaret have received their salaries?

ENTERPRISE START UP

Enterprise Start Up is the name chosen by a volunteer group of ex business and management students who hold monthly meetings to advise people thinking of starting their own businesses. The self help group was formed by Julie Constandinidou who was concerned at the lack of help for prospective business people. She and two other students formed ESU and have registered it as a charity. Prospective entrepreneurs are asked to make a donnation after their initial consulation but ESU does charge fees if entrepreneurs ask it to conduct business viability studies.

Last week Emma Botten approached ESU. She would like to set up a dress shop which would specalise in selling top quality materials, wool and other sewing equipment. Emma has had considerable experience in this type of work as she has been a pattern cutter for a large dress making firm. Her knowledge of the industry is good but she feels she lacks the necessary skills for runnning a business.

Emma has found what she believes are suitable premises but has limited financial resources. She needs to borrow £40,000 to purchase the property, some stock and still leave her with sufficient working capital. Emma has inherited her parent's house and is prepared to offer that as security. In addition she has £15,000 in a building society account which she is prepared to put into the business. She has read books about starting your own business but has come to see you to ask you the following questions.

1   How can I raise the additional capital I need to start my business?

2   Are there any government grants available to people like me?

3 What is a business plan and how would it help me to start my own business?

4 Where can I obtain information about starting my own business?

THE RIVER THAMES HOTEL

The River Thames Hotel is a new large hotel situated on the South Bank of the River Thames. It is set in four acres which have been landscaped to provide an attractive environment for visitors.

Since its opening the hotel has been fully booked. About sixty per cent of the hotel's customers are overseas visitors to London. The largest number of foreign visitors are from the U.S.A., West Germany and France but the firm has noticed an increase in visitors from the Far East particularly Japan.

The firm's management believe that with the coming of the single market in 1992 they will have a large increase in business customers from the other EEC countries. Market research projections have also predicted a large increase in tourists wishing to visit Britain.

As a result the firm's management have decided to expand the hotel by building an extension which will add a hundred extra bedrooms, a new conference hall and an extra restaurant. The cost of this extension has been financed by borrowing 6 million Deutsch Marks on the Euro Market. The loan will be repayable in 12 years time and the firm intends to set aside sufficient Sterling each year which will be converted into Deutsch Marks to repay the loan so that the effects of exchange rate fluctuations can be minimised.

1   What are the benefits to Britain of companies choosing to borrow foreign capital?

2   What effect does this type of borrowing have on the balance of payments?

3 What are the effects of tourism on a country's balance of payments?

4 What factors cause exchange rates to alter and what effect do such movements have on the hotel industry in Britain?

MANOR ESTATES

Manor Estates is a small firm of estate agents situated in Welshpool. The firm has just had its best financial year ever with commissions on the sales standing at an all time record helped by the large increase in property prices. Prices have been rising in the area as people have been leaving the overcrowded South Eastern corner of England and opting for a more tranquil setting in rural England. Many of the new-comers still work in London and comute there daily via the good rail service.

The firm has also recently diversified and now offers a range of financial services. In the past, would be purchasers needing a mortgage were referred to a building society or bank but now Manor Estates arranges all aspects of financing the new property. The low level of interest rates and the large increase in wages lead to this side of the firm's business expanding rapidly. With the passing of the Financial Services Act the firm decided to expand this area of its operations still further by offering financial advice to would be investors.

You are presently employed at Manor Estates as part of your work experience. The senior partner Mr. Giles has just come into the office carrying the morning paper which carries the headline "Bank of England gives signal to money markets to raise interest rates as Chancellor fears a rapid increase in the money supply." Mr. Giles exclaims, "How can the money supply be increasing, after all surely the Chancellor knows how much money the Bank of England has printed." Turning to you he says, "Can you explain to me?"

1 What constitutes money in our economy?

2 How does the government measure the money supply?

3 How can the money supply increase and why is the Chancellor so concerned that he is having to raise interest rates?

4 What effect will a rise in interest rates have on Mr. Giles's business?

(*n.b.* As markets vary according to conditions of supply and demand, this must be borne in mind when answering the questions).

THE ISLAND ECONOMY

You have been asked to advise the political leaders of a small island which is situated in the Pacific Ocean about two hundred miles North West of Australia. The island is about seventy square miles, has been endowed with a good climate for growing agricultural products and has two excellent harbours which have already been developed as ports.

The island's economy suffers from most of the problems of a developing third world country. It has to import nearly all of its raw materials, fuel and manufactured goods and has to pay for them by exporting its agricultural products to the USA, Australia and Japan. The price of agricultural products tend to fluctuate widely on the world market and this has led to the country having occasional balance of payments problems.

The leaders believe that there is a sound argument for borrowing international finance so that the economy can be transformed from an agricultural economy to an industrial one. Some people think that the island could become a new Taiwan. However, others are worried about spoiling the natural beauty of the island and believe that resources should not be switched from agriculture to industrialisation.

You have been given a table showing the present and forecast possible levels of GNP, employment, consumption and investment. You are to assume that the increase in GNP will be brought about by industrialisation, but also that the island's already large population is estimated to increase by 400 per cent in the next ten years.

Forecast Income and Expenditure Model

Year	GNP £m	Employment in millions	Consumption £m	Investment £m
1990	50	15	70	20
1991	100	20	110	20
1992	150	25	150	20
1993	200	30	190	20
1994	250	35	230	20
1995	300	40	270	20
1996	350	45	310	20
1997	400	50	350	20
1998	450	55	390	20
1999	500	60	430	20

1 Calculate the change in aggregate expenditure, the change in savings and the change in the level of stocks for each year.

2 At what level of GNP is the economy operating at equilibrium?

3 Why is it that the number of people employed in the economy is dependent on the level of GNP?

4 What will be the opportunity cost of industrialisation?

PAUL & NICOLA AUBREY

Paul and Nicola met at University. Nicola was studying computer programming and Paul was completing the last year of his post graduate certificate in education so that he could become a teacher.

They have been married for two years and they live in a terraced house in Leeds which they bought for £18,000. Paul teaches at a local school and Nicola works as a programmer for the local authority.

Last month Nicola saw a job advertised by a software house based in Burnham. The firm were looking for a graduate with one year's experience and were offering a salary of £16,000 plus a Ford Fiesta.

Nicola and Paul discussed the job and they decided that she should apply for it. A week later Nicola received a letter inviting her to attend an interview. At the interview she was amazed to be the only candidate and asked where the other candidates were. Her future manager replied "I'll be honest with you. We find it very difficult to recruit staff. There is a labour shortage here. We just can't recruit young graduates even though we are paying a reasonable salary. Once people look in the estate agents windows, they tell us that they can't afford to live here and we lose another applicant.

Still let's be positive. I would like to offer you the job but suggest you look at the house prices and think it over. I'll hold the job open for you for a fortnight."

Nicola thanked him and made her way to the station. Just outside she noticed a firm of estate agents. In the window were large detached houses which she knew they could not afford. As she entered she was greeted by a friendly young executive. Nicola told him that she had just been offered a job and that she was looking for a terraced house. She already had a house in Leeds which was now worth about £25,000.

The estate agent smiled. Well he said. " I'm afraid we do not have anything in that price range. Look, without being rude, you just can't afford to live here. In Bracknell, Reading or Slough you can still get a terraced house for about £60,000 but in Burnham we do not have any property in that price range. I can have details sent to you from our other offices if you like."

Nicola thanked him. She took the train back to Leeds. Even on her new salary, how could they afford it? When she told Paul he said, "Well, it's hopeless. We would be no better off and I do like it here." Nicola agreed. Why leave her home town if they would be no better off financially? The next day she phoned the firm and told the manager that they could not afford a house and could therefore not take the job.

1 What factors influence house prices in diffferent parts of the country?

2 What effect do high South of England house prices have on labour mobility?

3 What problems may firms experience in the South of England if house prices remain substantially higher than in the rest of the United Kingdom?

4 What action could governments take to try and increase labour mobility?

THE TRUCKERS' FRIEND

The Trucker's Friend is well equipped restaurant which specialises in cuisine for long distance lorry drivers. The owner James Thomas had been a long distance driver for many years and had realised that there was a need for this type of restaurant. Ten years ago he had married an Italian cook who had worked in a similar restaurant in Italy. James' idea was to run a restaurant which would appeal to both British and continental drivers by providing what he called the best of European food combined with a friendly service.

As night fell on a late November evening two trucks pulled into the restaurant lorry park. The drivers Alan and Robert greeted each other and began to walk into the restaurant.

James.   "Hello. Have you had a good day? Not too many hold ups I hope."

Alan.   "Yes I'm alright. Very hungry though. I'm really looking forward to some of your wife's excellent food."

Robert.   "Me too. This is about the only place in England that seems to understand truckers. Sometimes I think we're outcasts. Motorists seem to hate us and restaurants seem to think we have leprosy. Why else do they put up NO LORRIES signs."

Alan.   "Alright Robert. Don't go on. You know we're welcome here. Just relax."

James.   "Am I correct in thinking you'll both order your usual feast? If you want a change Gina has just made an excellent lasagne and our salads are very fresh."

Alan.	"Yes you tempt me. I must stop eating unhealthy food?
Robert.	"I'll stick with my usual, OK?"
James.	"Thank you. I'll take your order to the kitchen and then I'll come back for a chat. We're a bit quiet tonight."

James returns from the kitchen.

James.	"Your meals will be ready in about 20 minutes. How's your new truck Alan?"
Alan.	"I'm delighted with it. It was very expensive, £87,000, but it's worth its weight in gold and is so economical. I've just come back from Milan with a load of Italian men's suits and it was just a pleasure to drive it."
Robert.	"Yes. Alan has convinced me. Next time I too will be adding to the Balance of Payments problem. The Swedish trucks are so comfortable and their reliability and after sales service is excellent."
James.	"Things have certainly changed from my day. Then no one ever thought of buying a foreign truck and, as for Italian suits, well everything I buy now seems to come in from abroad. Last month we bought a new dishwasher and a new food blender both made in West Germany."
Alan.	"Yes I know. Every time I come back from the continent I think the same. An Italian driver said to me the other week that their Gross Domestic product is bigger than ours. So I said to him. 'That's good you can buy me the next drink.' Still it's serious really."

Robert. "When I first started in this job driving to Scotland was considered a long drive. People would have thought you were mad if you said you were driving to the Gulf. Now I do most of my runs there. For the last six months I have been delivering electronic components for their new radar system. Now they are made here James. I always say if they are not buying something from you, how can we buy something from them?"

James. "Yes I suppose you're right. I just can't get used to the fact that we now import more manufacured goods than we export. Ah! here comes my wife with your food. Well as they say in Italy, 'L'appetito viene manglando. (Eating gives you an appetite)'."

1 What contribution do Alan, James and Robert make to the United Kingdom's balance of payments?

2 What is a country's gross domestic product and how is it measured?

3 Does it matter that Britain is importing more manufactured goods than she exports?

4 Why do the balance of payments always balance?

JONQUIL FASHIONS

Jonquil Fashions is a small firm of dress makers in North London. The firm has two small lock up units where it manufactures ladies dresses which are sold to fashion boutiques all over the country. The firm employs twenty people who cut out and machine the fabric. Once a year pay rates are adjusted taking into account the level of inflation, competitors' pay rates and the demand and supply for machinists in the area. Jonquil Fashions have a reputation in the industry for paying higher wages because the firm has always wanted to attract the best machinists so that its clothes are always of consistent quality. Even so the directors know that their wages are low compared with the average industrial wage and have promised the work force that they will take steps to increase wages above the rate of inflation for the next three years. It is hoped that this policy will benefit the firm in 1992 if the European Community insist that Britain introduces minimum wage legislation. By increasing wages now the firm will be able to pass on its increased wage costs gradually thereby giving it a competitive edge over its rivals who do not adopt such a policy.

1 Why might the European Community wish to introduce minimum wage legislation?

2 What effect would minimum wage legislation have on the overall labour market?

3 What effect would minimum wage legislation have on Jonquil Fashion's business?

GOLDEN EAGLE KNITWEAR LTD

Golden Eagle Knitwear is a medium sized firm manufacturing a range of cashmere and lambswool pullovers and cardigans for both the male and female market. The firm was founded twenty years ago by Annie Shaw who had worked for many years in the Scottish woollen industry as a cost accountant.

Annie Shaw started the company with £10,000 and at first the firm only employed five people in a small industrial unit on the outskirts of Dundee. The firm's success lay in its ability to create attractive designs which always incorporated an eagle somewhere in the garment. Today the firm employs over a hundred people and its products are sold in the United States, West Germany and Japan.

Last year over 50% of sales came from abroad and the company is keen to increase its sales in the affluent foreign markets of the world. The firm's sales force regularly make business trips abroad to try to secure orders from fashion and department stores. It is a sales strategy which has proved to be very successful because the firm could not have enjoyed such rapid growth had it not been able to compete in overseas markets.

One factor which is always of concern to the Board of Directors is the exchange rate. If Sterling falls against the world's hard currencies there is a danger of an increase in price of raw materials which can increase the United Kingdom's inflation rate. This can lead to pressure from the work force for large pay rises which can increase the cost of each garment making them uncompetitive in the firm's main markets. Similarly a rise in the value of Sterling vis a vis the main currencies makes the firm's products more expensive compared with domestically produced products in the main export markets and can therefore lead to a loss of sales.

The workers at Golden Eagle Knitwear all receive profit sharing, so that their Christmas bonus is directly related to the firm's results. Annie Shaw always says. "What's good news for us is soon good news for our suppliers and other business people in the area". For the last five years the firm has been recruiting extra staff and the directors believe that their full order book will ensure that they will continue to be a recruiter of labour for next year. This is good news for a town which has seen quite high unemployment as many of the traditional industries in the area have declined. In the new year the company is going to be visited by the Secretary of State for Scotland as part of his tour of the area. They hope to gain valuable television and press coverage from the visit which will further boost sales in the coming year.

1 Why are export sales so important to the firm and to the town of Dundee?

2 What does Annie Shaw mean by, "What's good news for us is soon good news for other business people in the area?"

3 What factors cause the Sterling exchange rate to fluctuate on the foreign exchange markets?

4 If the United Kingom had a higher rate of inflation than that of its main industrial competitors what effect would it have on Golden Eagle's export sales?

MEDICAL RESEARCH

Medical Research specialise in manufacturing drugs for the treatment of tropical diseases. Two years ago one of their research scientists developed a drug codenamed 234 which is used in the treatment of malaria. It is the only one of its kind and the firm has obtained a patent for it which will last for the next fifteen years.

The company directors hope to be able to recoup the high development costs quickly and to take advantage of the monopoly position before their patent expires. As a result they have decided to appoint you as a consultant to help them achieve the most profitable cost to output ratio. The firm's costs and estimated sales for any given month are given below.

Quantity Per Month	Average Revenue	Total Revenue	Total Cost	ATC	MC	MR	NR
0	48		75,000				
1000	45		105,000				
2000	42		123,000				
3000	39		135,000				
4000	36		141,000				
5000	33		147,000				
6000	30		156,000				
7000	27		171,000				
8000	24		195,000				
9000	21		237,000				
10000	18		300,000				

The directors would like you to answer the following questions.

1 What is the most profitable level of output for the firm?

2 Draw a graph showing the firm's most profitable level of output.

3 What are the social implications if the firm decides to maximise production of the drug while it has the patent?

4 If the patent is not renewed what effect would other manufacturers marketing a similar drug have on the firm?

CANDMAR

Candmar are a Korean firm of transistor radio manufacturers. For years they have made and marketed cheap radios which have been sold in North America and Western Europe. Their marketing strategy was to produce tiny radios which could be powered by a single battery and which would give a reasonable sound. The radios proved popular with youngsters in the 1960's who wanted to listen to pop music when they were working or relaxing outdoors.

By the end of the 1960's the firm were facing increased competition from other Far Eastern manufacturers and so they decided to diversify and to produce more expensive products. Today Candmar make a range of household electronic products. The firm has invested heavily in research and now manufacturers a range of in car hi fi products which are sold in specialist shops. In addition the firm manufactures video recorders and compact disc players under licence from some of the major Japanese electronic giants and has become one of the largest electronic companies in Korea.

This success has been gained by securing access to the rich export markets of North America and Western Europe, principally the European Community. With the coming together of a single market in 1992 Candmar has decided to open its first overseas manufacturing plant on the outskirts of Liverpool. The firm has chosen the area because of its good communications and because it is near North Wales where a number of Korean and Japanese businesses have recently set up. Cheaper rents coupled with attractive government grants however meant that Candmar chose Liverpool instead of North Wales. The firm hopes to employ 100 workers initially and hopes to expand the factory by the end of the 1990's.

1 What grants are available to firms who are willing to create jobs in Liverpool?

2 Why is the government prepared to offer financial inducements to overseas firms such as Candmar?

3 What effect will such investment have on the UK economy?

4 Why do you think Candmar chose to invest in Liverpool?

THE MARSHALL GROUP PLC

The Marshall group is an established plc. Its main business activities are the design and manufacture of household cleaning tools. At its main factory in Clwyd it manufactures brushes, pails, mops, dustbins and a range of cleaning tools for the industrial market.

During its fifty year history the firm has diversified. In the late 1970's Marshalls bought a chain of ironmongers in the North West and purchased two contract cleaning companies. These acquisitions proved to be very successful and encouraged the management to consider other acquisitions.

In 1979 the firm called in a team of management consultants to see how the business could be further developed. The consultants reported that the cleaning market was at near saturation and that the firm could no longer enjoy steady growth by just continuing with this sector. The consultants 'advice was to diversify and to use the proceeds of the latest rights issue to purchase young fast growing companies in related businesses.

The Board of Directors believed that the best opportunities lay in the expanding DIY market. Market research showed that this market was growing rapidly and that the British spent more on their homes than any of their European counterparts. In 1983 Marshalls bought a paint manufacturer, a wallpaper manufacturer and obtained the exclusive franchise to market a range of Spanish wall tiles. The firm's aim was to promote these products in its own stores and to obtain additional distribution outlets from the large DIY retailers.

The Directors believed that it would take at least five years before they saw a healthy return from their investment but that they would see sales and profits grow steadily throughout that time. Unfortunately only the tile franchise has made money. The paint factory has lost money every year and the wallpaper manufacturer has only managed to break-even or produce small profits.

As a result Marshall's share price has underperformed on the stock exchange share index and shareholders have become pessimistic about the earnings potential of their shares. Marshall's directors have decided to sell off the paint and wallpaper and to concentrate instead on their existing core businesses and their tile franchise. They hope that this decision will improve their earnings per share and that the share price will recover, thereby making the shares attractive to existing and potential investors.

1 Why do firms seek to diversify and what name is given to this type of diversification?

2 Why is diversification sometimes less successful than the firm's management originally thought?

3 What factors affect the market price of a firm's shares?

4 Why is it important that Marshall's shares perform as well as the Financial Times Share Index?

FOOD & DRINK SUPPLIES

Food and Drink Supplies specalise in providing buffet meals for outside catering events. The firm has been established ten years and is situated in a busy part of North London with close proximity to the West End and the City.

The firm employs twenty five people. Five members of staff are engaged in food preparation and the other ten staff work as waiters once the food is delivered to customers. The remaining staff are employed either in administration or as drivers.

One of the firm's specialisms is in being able to arrange last minute catering facilities. They boast that within an hour staff can be on your premises offering guests a business buffet. This has proved a very popular sevice with many firms who have had to arrange important business meetings at very short notice. Every day the staff prepare extra food so that they can provide this specialist service.

Food and Drink Supplies have always been good employers. All of the staff are covered by the firm's pension scheme and are paid sick leave. In addition their wages are 10% higher than the industry average. However, in spite of these benefits the firm has recently been experiencing a high rate of labour turnover amongst its younger staff. This has meant that the firm's management have had to spend an increased amount of their time on recruitement, and the constant staff changes have had an effect on staff morale. The directors are worried that the constant staff changes will have an adverse effect on their business and are wondering what they should do. They have asked you to advise them and have asked you the following questions.

1 What factors generally lead to a high rate of labour turnover in an industry?

2 What factors should the management consider if they are trying to motivate their staff?

3 Why might a good benefits package fail to motivate staff?

IRON STONE CHINA LTD

Iron Stone China is a well established china manufacturer situated in the West Midlands. For well over a hundred and fifty years the company has produced all sorts of china for both the industrial and consumer market. The firm is a large exporter with over 30% of its sales being to the USA, Canada and West Germany.

The firm's directors are anxious to make the most of the single European market. They have appointed a team of management consultants to advise them about which products they would be best to concentrate on and how they should go about securing distribution outlets in other EC countries. They are particularly keen to sell products in the growing Italian market.

The consultants have just prepared a major report for the firm which they have called A Strategic Plan for the 1990's. In the plan the consultants have analysed current and future markets, and have outlined areas where they believe the firm could expand. The plan also outlines what the future strategy should be and the future mission.

The directors are very pleased with the report and are committed to putting its recommendations into action. At their last meeting it was decided to book the local town hall and invite all of the staff to explain to them the firm's new strategy for the single European Market. You have been given the task of arranging the presentation and have been asked to give a talk explaining the following points to the work force.

1 What is meant by the term strategy and how does it differ from a plan?

2 What is a firm's mission statement and why is it important that the workers know what it is?

3 What benefits does the firm gain by writing a corporate plan?

4 What action should the company's management take to ensure that future events conform to their plan?

REDUNDANCIES AT SWAN GLASS

Swan Glass is a medium sized firm who specalise in cut glass, vases, glasses and other ornaments. The firm are just about to hold their emergency Directors meeting.

James Ferguson, Managing Director. "Good morning, I'm sure you all know why I have called this emergency meeting. I will ask our Sales Director to bring us up to date on all the facts."

Beverley Roberts, Sales Director. "Thank you James. It is indeed bad news. You know that we were tendering to supply the French chain of shops Les Magasins with our cut glass vases. I'm afraid I have to tell the Board that we have not won the contract and that our existing contract expires at the end of February. With the market the way it is there is no way that we can sell the extra capacity to our existing customers."

Production Director, George Harvey. "Well, I suppose I can transfer some of my glass cutters to work on the other product ranges. They are all skilled workers and it has taken me years to build up such a team of effective workers."

James Ferguson. "No Alan. I'm afraid that is not possible. Your glass cutting department is losing money every week. When times were better we could afford to carry the odd lame duck but not any more. This time we are going to have to make thirty glass cutters redundant."

George Harvey. "That will cut my work force by 60% in that area of operations. I don't know what it will do to morale. Many of the workers have been expecting bad news. They have seen the stock building up in the warehouse and we all know what that means. But this is even worse than the factory rumour. Still, can't something be done to save my section?"

Julia Bates, Finance Director. "I'm sorry Alan. I 've had my chief accountant analyse all of our costs. We are not even breaking even in that market segment any more. Other countries seem able to make cut glass cheaper than we can and we must capitalise on our other ranges which can still stand up to the international competition. If we make those people redundant the rest of the firm stands a chance of getting back onto a stronger financial footing. I know the area has a high rate of unemployment but unless we take drastic action now we could lose the whole firm. You know that in the third quarter we made a trading loss of £140,000 which completely wiped out the other two quarters' profit.

George Harvey. "Yes, I know, but I hate to lose such good and effective workers. You know that we have had no industrial relations problems in this factory and that our labour turnover is vey low amongst our skilled workers. It just all seems to be a terrible waste that's all."

Peter Smith, Personnel Director. "I have been through our personnel records. Fortunately the average age in that Department is 47 and so many of the workers are approaching retirement. I propose that we tell the workers that redundancies are inevitable but that in the first instance they will be voluntary. We have always done it this way in the past and I for one would hate to see us break that precedent. I have worked out with Julia a financial package which I believe will be both attractive to our staff and the company. The details are contained in my report which was circulated to you last week."

James Ferguson. "Well, is the Board unanimous in accepting the proposal that thirty redundancies are inevitable but that they will

be voluntary in the first instance? Good, then that is decided.
Peter will you arrange to have details of the scheme put in all our
employees' pay packets. Let's hope we don't lose any of our
younger staff."

1 Why are firms forced to make staff redundant?

2 What effect will these further redundancies have on the local
   community?

3 In the statistics the workers who are made redundant are just
   unemployed, but how do economists distinguish between different types of unemployment?

4 What action can the government take to help the unemployed
   glass workers find new employment?

BIRMINGHAM METAL PRODUCTS

For the last seventy years Birmingham Metal Products have manufactured a range of products for the construction industry. The main products are nails, screws, bolts, hinges and brackets which are sold to builders merchants, and large DIY stores. The firm employs over one hundred and fifty people at its Birmingham factory and its present organisation system has remained the same since the last managing director took the advice of a firm of managment consultants and installed a functional organisation chart.

When this was done there was some resistance to the new organisation. In the past the firm had been run by the founding family but when it went public in the late 1950s a new team of directors were appointed, and the founder's grandchildren chose other careers. The original family still own 30% of the share capital but no longer play any part in the day to day management of the firm.

During the last ten years Birmingham Metal Products has been facing increased competition from foreign manufacturers. Most of the imports come from the new developing economies in the Far East but in recent years the firm has noticed that many of the large bolts used in constructing high-rise buildings are made in Germany.

During the last recession the firm saw many of the traditional metal related businesses in the West Midland go bankrupt. The once large industrial estates became large waste lands and for the first time in over fifty years the area experienced high concentrations of unemployment. Birmingham Metal Products were fortunate in having built up a thriving export business with most of the products being sold to Italy, Oman and Kuwait. With 1992 approaching the directors have decided to consolidate on their exporting success by purchasing an Italian manufacturer of construction products on the outskirts of Milan. The aim of the purchase is to give the firm a strong presence in the EC once the single market comes into operation.

The Board of Directors are considering the re-organisation of their company. They are worried that their functional organisation system which is in operation in both countries is unsuitable for present market conditions. Also, recently, there have been a number of communication problems between the two factories. They have appointed you as a freelance consultant to advice them on changing their organisational structure and have asked you the folowing questions.

1 What are the main organisational problems in operating two manufacturing operations in different parts of Europe?

2 Is a functional organisation system the most suitable for their type of business? What other systems could the firm consider?

3 What would be the advantages in decentralising responsibility from Birmingham to Milan?

THE CHEMICAL COMPANY

The directors of the Chemical Company are becoming increasingly concerned about their company's attitude towards the environment. In the past the firm like most of the other industry in the Midlands did not concern itself too much with the effects of pollution. As a result toxic chemicals were pumped into the local rivers and large quantities of carbon dioxide were pumped daily into the sky.

For many years now the Board of Directors at the firm have been developing a strategy for reducing pollution. The problem is that as long as there is a demand for toxic products hazardous waste will be created, but the firm now take a much more responsible attitude than they did in the past. The current "Green" movement coupled with EC directives have made the directors consider a new strategy for the 1990's. The directors have invited lecturers from the local Polytechnic to advise them on how to install additional pollution controls and the firm have budgeted an extra £750,000 a year to be spent on this type of work. The directors hope that this will make them one of the greenest chemical companies in the country and that this will enhance the future image and sales of the company?

1 Why do firms develop corporate strategies?

2 What should the firm do to ensure that its new strategy is successfully implemented?

3 What macro factors should the firm consider before developing its new corporate strategy?

RECYCLED PAPER PRODUCTS

Recycled Paper Products is a medium sized family business. The company has been owned by the family for nearly fifty years although they no longer manage it, preferring to leave its day-to-day operations to the Board of Directors. Since the retirement of the last managing director the firm needs to appoint a new managing director. The present Board of Directors would like to see the company expand at a faster rate and to exploit the coming opportunities which the new single market will bring.

The company owns its five acre site on the outskirts of Newcastle and has net assets of £1.75 million. It also has a healthy cash balance of £200,000 which is currently invested in short term Government stock, and last year the firm employed a hundred people.

The Board of Directors have approached a firm of recruitmemt consultants. The Board would ideally like to appoint someone who is about thirty-five years of age and who has experience of being a company director. The successful applicant should be professionally qualified preferably with an MBA and have experience of working in the paper and packaging industry.

The recruitment agency have just phoned to inform you of this vacancy. They believe that your background and qualifications make you an ideal choice. As part of the initial interviews you have agreed to meet the directors and give a short presentation on the company's future business objectives. The consultants have told you that your talk should last for ten minutes after which there will be a short period for questioning. Formal interviews are planned for the following week.

THE TRAINEE MANAGER

You work as a trainee journalist on a local newspaper. Your editor is keen to feature articles which will appeal to young readers and so once a month the paper features an article entitled Career Matters. By the time this week's edition is published the 'A' Level results will have been issued and many school leavers will be deciding whether or not to start careers as management trainees or to continue with their education by taking courses at Polytechnics and Universities.

Your editor Sharon Clark has asked you to write an article of about 1,500 words on the subject of management. She believes that the word management means different things to different people but that if school leavers are going to become management trainees they should have an understanding of what a career in management will involve.

WOODLAND FURNITURE

Woodland Furniture is a medium sized firm of furniture manufacturers. It has been in existence for nearly twenty-five years and during that time it has built up a reputation for good quality furniture. Unlike most of its competitors, the firm has never manufactured flat-pack furniture believing that the consumer prefers to pay a little more for a perfectly finished product. The company always uses traditional materials and it introduced fire resistant coverings and foam long before it became a legal requirement. This has given the firm valuable publicity with the result that several large furniture stores placed orders for the firm's products. However most of the firm's furniture was sold to small family owned furniture shops in the South East of England.

In an attempt to secure more retailing space Woodland Furniture purchased a chain of furniture stores in the West Midlands. The boom in the housing market had greatly increased the demand for all types of furniture and Woodland Furniture's factory had been working at near capacity. In some cases customers were having to wait up to three months before they could be promised delivery and the new stores were able to sell their stock as soon as they received it. In an attempt to reduce customer waiting time the firm had started work on building a new 30,000 square feet of additional factory space and had purchased new machine tools from West Germany and Sweden. Unfortunately, when the new extension became operational, the firm found itself in a different market. Interest rates had been raised and the boom in the housing market had all but come to an end. Woodland Furniture now found itself with extensive debt and falling sales.

Woodland Furniture's management knew that their main customers were young people aged between twenty-four and thirty-five. They liked the firm's designs and found that the furniture was attractively priced. This age range accounted for nearly sixty per cent of the firm's sales causing concern at such heavy dependence on one buyer segment. One of the main reasons for purchasing the new stores was to try and appeal to older customers by displaying more expensive products in some of the new outlets. The hope was that by trying to appeal to additional market segments the firm could reduce its dependence on one main market segment and move into the more profitable areas of the furniture market.

Unfortunately, the furniture market was severely depressed by the time these new products were available, but consumer reaction was favourable and the firm is enjoying a better level of sales than many of its rivals even though turnover and profits are below budget. In an attempt to conserve working capital the firm reduced its dividend payments and approached its bankers about rescheduling some of its short term debt.

During the current financial year the company is continuing with its strategy of trying to appeal to older, more affluent consumers. It has destocked and reduced the work force by five per cent. It has so far avoided the temptation of price cutting and hopes that the following year will see a reduction in interest rates and an improvement in the housing market which would leave the firm well placed to benefit from its recent expansion programme.

1 What are Woodland Furniture's main strengths and weaknesses?

2 What are the major macro economic factors affecting the firm?

3 How important are demographic trends to Woodland Furniture?

4 Is it possible for the firm's management to control the environmental factors which affect the company?

DRAGON TILES

Dragon Tiles are a medium sized firm of ceramic tile manufacturers in North Wales. The firm has taken its name from the Welsh mythical animal and uses the symbol of a red dragon on a green background as its brand name. The recent boom in the housing market has meant that the firm has been enjoying large production runs and that overtime working has been necessary to be able to keep up with demand. This has lead to the need for additional warehousing space and has brought about a complete review of the firm's stock holding policy.

In the past the company managed with a manual system of stock control but the recent increase in business has meant that such a system has been unable to cope with the number of orders. Internally the Board of Directors acknowledge that their stock control is not as efficient as it should be and that it could lead to the firm losing orders. At present five people are employed in the warehouse and the average age of the workforce is forty-five.

The directors of Dragon Tiles have decided to install a computer to help them with stock control and their aim is to redeploy two of the workers in the factory. By computerising the warehouse they hope to be able to reduce costs and provide customers with a more efficient delivery system. A firm of consultants have been appointed to design and install the new system but the directors are worried as to how the workforce will view the change. In the past changes in work practices have sometimes led to staff leaving the company or opting to take early retirement.

You work as a free lance consultant specalising in personnel matters and have been asked the following questions by the Directors of Dragon Tiles.

1 What steps should the directors take before instigating the new system?

2 Why may staff be reluctant to take part in organisational change?

3 In what way do market forces necessitate organisational change?

METAL ENGINEERING LTD

It is Monday morning at Metal Engineering Ltd and Diana Shields the Personnel Director is preparing her papers for the Board meeting to discuss next year's training budget. Diana knows that the company prefers to spend its money on new capital equipment because several of the directors believe that they can always hire the people they need by recruiting staff from other firms. At 8.30a.m. the meeting begins. The Managing Director John Prescott is in the chair, and the Marketing Director Peter Brown, Finance Director Gemma Thomas and Production Director Secretary David Alford are already seated.

John Prescott. " Good Morning everybody. Thank you all for being here so early. We've got a lot to do, so let's get started. I have ordered morning coffee and toast and that should be here any time now. Well Gemma have you finished all the budgets?"

Gemma Thomas. "Yes. I have had copies of the draft budgets prepared. They are similar to last year with the exception of a £50,000 staff development and training budget. Diana has begun to convince me that it makes financial sense. Last year we spent over £15,000 on recruitment costs and our labour turnover rate was over 30% in some areas."

Diana Shields. "Thank you Gemma. I have been carrying out a major survey of our future personnel requirements. If the firm keeps on growing at its present rate we are going to need to recruit an additional 10% more staff each year for the next five years and this figure assumes that none of our present staff resign. Obviously that is unrealistic, but the demographic changes mean that we are no longer going to have access to a pool of untrained young school leavers. In the future more of our employees are likely to be female and the average age of the firm's employees is bound to increase. As a result I believe it makes sense to introduce a staff development programme and encourage staff to acquire the new skills which we will need in the 1990's."

John Prescott. "Sometimes I think there is a conspiracy going on. In the past we have never had to waste money on these things. I have invested thousand of pounds in new plant and machinery with the aim of reducing personnel in this organisation so that the accompanying labour problems can be reduced. I know we have trained our own engineers but that has always been the exception. Where is the money coming from, that is what I want to know?"

David Alford. " I know how you feel John. In the past I always thought the same. Why train staff when you only lose them to other employers, but Diana has started to convince me about the soundness of her arguments. I have not been able to recruit a trainee company secretary because we won't give day release and Gemma knows that we can no longer recruit the trainee accounting staff which we need. Also we must ensure that our engineers have the best skills so that we can still continue to compete with our German and Italian competitors."

John Prescott. "Oh no David. Please don't go on again about the state of the United Kingdom's manufacturing industry. It worries me too. Before long we'll be a nation of theme parks and museums. God knows how the country will survive then. Tell me more about your proposal then Diana."

Diana Shields. "Well I would like to spend £50,000 on allowing our staff to attend courses so that they can acquire new qualifications and gain greater experience. I would like to see all of our young staff being allowed day release and in the areas of key shortages such as electrical engineering and accountancy I would like to see us train any member of staff regardless of age whom we think would benefit from such a course."

Gemma Thomas. "I think she's right John. You know I never believe in spending money unless we get a good return. It's hard to measure the return from spending on staff. It isn't like working out the returns from a new piece of machinery. But without the staff where would we be?"

John Prescott. "Well maybe you're right. Never had these terms for myself, but having listened to the arguments I think we should introduce such a programme. From the conversations here today I take it that everyone else is agreed. Well let's move onto the next topic."

1 What effect will the demographic trends have on enterprise?

2 How should the firm begin to carry out an effective personnel planning policy?

3 Why is it important for companies to invest money in training?

4 What effect do you think the new policy will have on the firm's workers?

AMALGAMATED METAL PRODUCERS

AML celebrated its half centenary last year. The company had originally been founded to manufacture sheet metal which it sold to local engineering firms. It had stayed in this market until the sixties when it began to see profits and sales decline as imports took an ever increasing share of the market. In 1966 the firm started to diversify and to concentrate on producing relatively cheap items which are purchased by thousands of companies such as bolts, washers, screws, brackets and nails. By the middle seventies the firm had ceased producing sheet metal because high import penetration had reduced profits in this sector dramatically. AML had also altered its channels of distribution. In the past it only sold its products to the industrial market but now 40% of sales are in the lucrative DIY market. This meant that when the firm lost industrial orders in the recession of the 1980's (when interest rates were high and Sterling strong) it was still able to supply the consumer market, thereby helping it to survive the recession.

As part of the policy of diversification the company has just acquired a small firm of brush manufacturers. AML intends to sell these products to both its industrial and DIY outlets and hopes that the shift away from its traditional products will benefit it in the future.

1 Why do marketers distinguish between industrial and consumer markets?

2 What are the major problems to the firm in marketing a new product?

3 How do high interest rates affect AML's business activity?

4 What effect does a high exchange rate have on AML's export sales?

DRIVE IN

The Drive In petrol chain own and operate five garages selling petrol and other sundries in South London. All of the garages are situated on busy roads but there is a lot of competition from other companies in the area.

The last few years have seen a decline in profit margins on petrol and the firm has had to augment its profits by selling a range of goods which appeal to motorists and local consumers in the area.

Every year the firm holds its management conference in Bournemouth so that the company can formulate its business plan for the coming year. Drive In would like to increase its profits from its main business which is selling petrol. The managers know that the key to profitability lies in raising the price which they charge for petrol. Unfortunately competitors are either unwilling or reluctant to raise the price and so Drive In has to adopt the same pricing policy as its competitors.

1 What type of market do Drive In operate in?

2 What are the characteristics of this type of market?

3 Explain why Drive In's management cannot improve their profitability on petrol sales by altering the price of petrol unilaterally?

4 What would be the best methods of promoting the firm's petrol?

THE DIY HIRE SHOP

The DIY Hire Shop was set up three years ago with the aim of hiring out expensive items which customers need for major DIY tasks around the house. At first the firm stocked items like Kango drills, cement mixers, and scaffolding but soon found that customers were prepared to hire anything from a pick to a wheel barrow. The business has grown and the owners are looking at new ways of expanding their business.

One of their ideas is to add garden tools to their list of hire equipment. They are considering starting with motor lawn mowers and then expanding the range of tools if they are successful. The directors are not certain what price to charge for a day's hire. They believe that the lawn mowers will be as popular as their aluminium extension ladders and are considering purchasing twelve machines. The figures for the hire charge and estimated demand are shown below.

Daily Hire Charge	Estimated Demand
£10	10
£ 8	20
£ 6	40
£ 4	70
£ 2	120

1 Draw a graph showing the demand curve for the lawn mowers.

2 Why does the demand schedule slope downwards from left to right and what does this mean for the firm when selecting its pricing strategy?

3 What would be the optimum price for the firm to charge with its present number of machines?

4 How can the firm alter the demand curve by changing the variables in the marketing mix?

WINSLOW CHURCH

Last year Winslow Church celebrated its nine hundred year anniversary. The village of Winslow was mentioned in the Doomsday Book and there has been a church in the village since Saxon times. The Normans built a small stone church and over the centuries it has been extended and added to. In 1810 a spire was added and during that century several beautiful stained glass windows were installed.

The village population has remained stable since the 1970's. The local authority has declared the area a preservation zone and no new development is permiited. This has pleased villagers but has meant that the church's congregation has remained stable.

For many years now the roof has been in a poor state of repair. The vicar has commisioned a local firm of surveyors and they have reported that the spire and roof are in need of immediate attention. Some attention will also have to be paid to the stone walling and the entire cost has been put at £250,000.

You live in the area and work for a large fmcg company as a marketing director. In the last issue of the parish magazine you read that the vicar is appealing for a marketeer to help launch a restoration fund. You have written offering help and have just received the following reply.

The Vicarage
Winslow

Dear Chris Brooks

Thank you so much for your letter offering to help raise funds to restore our church. We are holding a meeting on the last Friday of this month and I would be pleased if you could speak to our parishioners on the following matters.

1　Why is it necessary to market the church?

2　How should we go about promoting our campaign?

3　What action should we take to raise the money?

4　What exactly is a public relations campaign?

I look forward to seeing you at the meeting.

God Bless

Gordon Brown

Gordon Brown

Vicar

ALL WOODS LTD

All woods is a medium sized firm of timber merchants. About 80 per cent of sales are to the construction industry with the balance being bought by DIY enthusiasts.

During the last five years the company has experienced an ever increasing demand for both soft and hard woods. This has meant constant sales and profits growth. Most of the soft woods are imported from Scandinavian countries and the USSR, but the hardwoods have to come from the tropical rain forests of Brazil and South East Asia. Modern double glazing techniques and the recent fashions in house and office design have greatly increased the demand for hardwoods. This has caused prices to rise and at times the firm has found it difficult to secure supplies. The directors of All Woods have recently visited several South East Asian countries with the aim of securing supplies from local merchants.

On the Directors' arrival back to the United Kingdom they were surprised to find that the company had become the subject of a headline in the local paper. The article accused the firm's Directors of damaging the environment by placing orders for hardwoods in countries which had already cut down large areas of forest. The article went on to ask if the world's ozone layer might be damaged for the sake of hardwood window frames and staircases?

The Directors are concerned that such adverse publicity could damage the business and are currently considering what action to take. They would like you to advise them on the following matters.

1 Is it possible for the firm to be environmentally conscious in its day-to-day trading?

2 Why do you think consumers and businesses are becoming so concerned about the environment?

3 What action should the Directors take in view of the newspaper article?

FIRST TIME HOMES

First Time Homes are a firm which specialise in building starter homes and flats in Britain. The firm realised that the starter home market was a growing market segment and decided to concentrate all of its resources on it.

During the last couple of years the firm has enjoyed very buoyant market conditions. Prospective customers have been prepared to place deposits as soon as the promotional brochures have been ready, in the belief that house prices can only rise.

The directors of First Time Homes have been working very hard to satisfy what at times has seemed to them to be a never-ending demand. They have scoured the South East of England looking for plots of land. Most of their land has been bought from suburban home owners who have been willing to sell off part of their large gardens for development.

With land prices steadily increasing the firm has tried to build up a large land bank so that it would not be held up while the market was so buoyant. This new land was financed by bank borrowings. In the past this had been profitable because interests rates were low and the pay back time was quick as the houses sold very quickly. However, today, it is a different story. The firm is finding it very difficult to sell houses now that interests rates have risen.

The finance director has become worried about the current financial position. Last week he had an appointment with the bank manager who expressed concern about the company's high borrowing. All of the loans had been taken out by offering the company's land bank as security. Land prices have subsequently fallen by 20 per cent and, as a result, the bank manager requires the firm to either reduce the loans or offer more security. The finance director has decided that the firm must construct and sell its three existing developments as quickly as possible and then slow down its rate of development in the coming year. This will allow the firm to reduce its borrowing while still allowing the company to keep its land bank for when market conditions improve.

To assist the firm in it task of selling houses quicker a new Marketing Diretor Julie Hull has been appointed. She has experience of marketing a wide range of products from cosmetics to industrial solvents.

Julie knows that her first task is to select suitable promotional techniques to encourage prospective purchasers to buy the firm's houses. She knows that this is not going to be easy. In the past the firm has been able to sell its houses before they were even built and regardless of quality. One of the sales force had told her "We don't sell houses, we ration them." Julie was shocked at this statement and has realised that her sales force will have to be retrained so that they have a thorough understanding of the marketing concept and how to apply it when selling houses.

You work for the company as a trainee marketing manager and Julie has asked you to prepare a report for her next Board of Directors' meeting.

1 What factors influence the demand for houses?

2 What incentives could the firm offer to buyers to try to offset the impact of high interest rates?

3 What is the marketing concept and how can it be applied to house building?

4 What has been wrong with the firm's selling policy?

THE FAMILY BUDGET

In 1980 Janice and Robert Curtis got married and a year later they had their first child Emma. Since then the family have kept detailed records of their total income and expenditure. The figures are given below.

Year	Income	Consumption
1981	12,000	11,500
1982	9,057	12,400
1983	10,700	13,459
1984	11,270	13,876
1985	17,800	14,369
1986	19,500	15,673
1987	22,400	17.975
1988	25,600	22,500
1989	28,900	26,783

1 From the above data calculate the family's;

        Average Propensity to Consume

        Average Propensity to Save

        Marginal Propensity to Consume

        Marginal Propensity to Save

2 Write a letter to Janice and Robert Curtis explaining the data which you have calculated.

3 Why is the level of consumer disposable income important to marketing management?

4 What sources of secondary data would you use to find out different levels of consumer income in Britain?

THE HAPPY HOUR

Catherine and Paul Yeoman own the Anvil and Hammer pub in a small village in Somerset. At the week end the pub does a good trade but Monday and Tuesday evenings are very quiet. The owners have been trying to think of ways to increase their takings on these two days and have decided to have a happy hour on each evening between the hours of 7pm and 8 pm when they will reduce the price of all of their draft beers which usually sell at a £1 a pint. They have estimated below how many pints they would serve during the happy hour at the following prices and still make a profit.

Price Per Pint	Quantity Sold
98p	27
95p	30
93p	35
91p	40
89p	45
87p	50
85p	60

1 Draw a demand schedule for the pub's happy hour.

2 What does a demand schedule tell the owners?

3 What is the law of demand and how does its operation affect the happy hour at the Anvil and Hammer?

4 How important is price as a marketing variable?

THE HANDSAW COMPANY

For many years the Handsaw company have marketed a range of hacksaws which have been sold mainly to builders' merchants. The saws have a good reputation and sell well under the brand name of Handsaw. The firm has seen sales grow at a steady rate but is concerned that unless it can manufacture and market other products it will see its sales and market share decline. To this end it has developed a new range of saws for cutting wood. The company is seeking to market these products to the industrial market and also to try to make inroads into the growing consumer and DIY market. Four new saws will be launched in total. They will all be made of the best steel and will have solid ash handles. Every saw will be guaranteed for three years and the advertisements will stress the quality of the new products. The advertisements will also stress that these saws are for the professional and that although the products are expensive they should be regarded as an investment.

The Directors of the Handsaw company are confident that they can secure shelf space in builders' merchants. Their products already have a good name and market research studies have shown that there is demand. It is the launching of the product onto the consumer market which is causing the marketing team the most concern, as most of their expertise has been in marketing individual products.

With two months to go before the launch of the new saws onto the consumer market the marketing team are currently researching the type of buyer who purchases good quality hand tools. The directors believe that the launch would be most successful if they could segment the market and aim the new products at a particular type of customer.

could segment the market and aim the new products at a particular type of customer.

1 What are the benefits to the Handsaw Company of segmenting the consumer market?

2 How could the firm segment the market?

3 What market reseach data would be useful to the firm when deciding how to segment the market?

4 What are the benefits to the firm of promoting the new saws under a new brand name in the consumer market?

GARDEN FURNITURE PRODUCTS

For over forty years Garden Furniture Products have built quality garden furniture using the finest teak woods. Their products have acquired a good name in both the United Kingdom and abroad. For the last three years the firm's turnover has been steady at about 1.25 million but the firm has seen its pre-tax profits fall by about 20% over the last three years.

The Marketing Director Angela Booth believes that this is because the firm's traditional products are reaching the end of their life cycle. Research has shown that consumers are becoming more price sensitive and are concerned about the deforestation and the use of hard woods for garden furniture. Metal and plastic garden furniture is becoming more popular with consumers although the industrial market still prefers wooden furniture.

Angela Booth believes that consumers still prefer wooden furniture but that high prices have led them to look at alternatives. As a result a new range of furniture has been developed made from softwoods which have been specifically designed for the smaller garden or apartment balcony. The products all come with a five year guarantee and cost about 20% more than their metal or plastic counterparts. The new range has been shown to department stores and garden centres and the initial reaction from buyers has been good. It is hoped that when the new range of products is launched in the Spring sales will be encouraging and that the firm will see an improvement in both its sales and profits. Angela Booth has told the Board of Directors that they should remain cautiously optimistic and that the firm should consider diversifying into making household wooden furniture in the future.

1 What is meant by the term the product life cycle?

2 In what ways can Garden Furniture Products extend the product life cycle for its products?

3 Why is it difficult to launch a successful new product onto the market?

4 Why are companies often reluctant to withdraw products which have come to the end of their life cycle?

THE WINDMILL

In 1979 Tara and Oliver Giles decided to purchase a disused windmill in Norfolk. Their original aim was to apply for planning permission to restore it and turn it into a family home. The Giles had lived in Kent for over ten years and they had seen derelict oast houses turned into fashionable family homes. Over the decade prices had risen and Mr and Mrs Giles believed that old windmills in Norfolk offered the same potential.

The windmill was in a dreadful state of disrepair. It had belonged to a farmer who had used it as a temporary barn. The farmer had agreed to sell it with five acres of land but had insisted that the buyer bought it on an, as is, where is basis. This meant that the first task was to remove all of the rubbish and old farm equipment which the farmer had left before initial renovation work could begin.

The surveyor who inspected the property estimated that the windmill would need £30,000 spending on it to turn it into an attractive home, and that an extra £10,000 would be required to build a small extension in the grounds. The Giles approached their local bank manager in Kent who was keen to lend on the property. The bank manager suggested that there might be a demand from tourists to see a working windmill and told Mr and Mrs Giles that she would be happy to finance the new machinery with a bank corporate term loan.

Mr and Mrs Giles didn't take the suggestion seriously at the time. They wanted a house not a living museum and were relieved to know that the bank were prepared to finance the refurbishment so that they could resell the property at a profit in about two years' time.

The following year saw the chances of a quick profit disappear. The economy was in a recession and interest rates were at an all time high. Oliver Giles was constantly worried about being made redundant. He worked for a large paper manufacturer in North Kent and the firm was losing money and orders in 1980. In 1981 Oliver was made redundant when the firm finally decided to close the factory. North Kent was beginning to look like a northern town with unemployment rising and factories closing. Oliver soon found that his skills were not needed and the redundancy payments were beginning to be eroded by the high mortgage repayments on their house in Kent and on the windmill.

During the winter of 1980 the Giles considered what they should do. Fortunately Mrs Giles was in work and her steady income as a legal executive for a local solicitor prevented the family from real financial hardship. They began to consider the bank manager's suggestion of making the windmill a tourist attraction but their initial research suggested that its location did not make this an ideal proposition on its own. However, if the windmill could be made to work, and if a bakery could be added to the site, this, plus tourism, could make the project a viable business.

Mr and Mrs Giles approached their bank manager to discuss their proposal. The bank manager suggested that they sold their house and lived in a caravan by the windmill while the work was being carried out. The manager said that the bank could not lend any more money until the windmill was restored but that then they would be prepared to lend 60% of the windmill's property value.

1981 was not an easy year to sell a house. High interest rates and local unemployment was making the market very stagnant. The local estate agent told them that a buyer could be found if their house was realistically priced for a quick sale. The Giles agreed and within three months they had sold their house and were able to commence restoring the windmill.

In order to restore the mechanical parts the Giles had to go to Holland. There were no longer any British manufacturers left but the Dutch firm assured Mr and Mrs Giles that they could undertake the work and that they could have the machinery in operation within six months of signing the contract.

Unemployment in the Norfolk area had also increased. This meant that when the Giles' planning application was submitted to the local authority it was looked on favourably as it would create jobs in construction and later jobs at the windmill.

By 1983 the Windmill Bakery Company was fully operational and employing four people. In the summer tourists came and paid to look around and photograph the windmill. The firm's main business was turning local wheat into flour and then producing small granary loaves which were sold to local shops.

Alhough the bakery was small it was able to be very economic because it used very little fuel. The windmill generated all of the power which gave the firm a 30% reduction in costs.

By 1986 the Windmill Bakery was employing twelve people. Demand for the firm's products was growing steadily. The firm had decided to capitalise on the "Green revolution" by only using wheat which had been grown using organic fertilisers. The large farms on the fens were not interested in producing wheat this way but small farms were attracted by the higher price per ton and began supplying the bakery direct instead of selling their grain to local merchants. The bakery also listed on the packet where the wheat was grown and gave an undertaking that it was free from any artificial fertilisers.

In 1987 the company had begun to sell its loaves to two of the large supermarket chains. The firm was now employing just over a hundred personnel and a management structure had just been introduced. Success was now beginning to bring new problems for Mr and Mrs Giles. They had to decide whether or not to limit the growth of their company by refusing additional orders, to sell it, or to raise additional finance so that the business could be expanded.

By 1988 Mr and Mrs Giles had decided to raise additional finance for the company and to expand its operations. They needed to raise an additional twelve million pounds. Part of the new capital would be used to reduce the firm's costly overdraft but most of the money would be invested in building a second windmill and acquiring an additional bakery.

The firm's accountants advised the Directors that they would be wise to consider issuing shares in the company on the Unlisted Securities Market. The Windmill Bakery met the criteria for this market but lacked all of the qualifications necessary for a full listing on the Stock Exchange. The company would receive the additional finance for expansion and Mr and Mrs Giles would be made millionares by virtue of their shareholding in the company.

The Directors agreed to seek a listing in 1990 and spent a large part of their time in 1989 visiting their Merchant Bankers and discussing ther new issue. In July 1990 the advertisements appeared inviting applicants to subscribe for the new shares. The Merchant Bank had agreed to underwrite the whole issue but had stressed all along that a successful launch depended upon investor confidence and good publicity.

The quality Sunday papers reviewed the Windmill Bakery and gave favourable press coverage. City analysts believed that this was a company that could continue to enjoy spectacular growth and that it was probably one of the most attractive companies coming to the market in 1990. In fact the launch was so successful that the applications for the shares were three times oversubscribed and investors had to have their applications scaled down. The company could have raised £36 million instead of the twelve million it required and began planning how the money should be invested.

1 What is the Unlisted Securities Market?

2 Why is it so important for new companies to be able to have their shares quoted on a stock market?

3 What factors lead to investor confidence when subscribing for shares?

4 What role to merchant banks play in financing industrial investment in Britain?

THE CHAIRPERSON'S STATEMENT

"Good morning, my Lords, Ladies and Gentlemen. It gives me great pleasure to announce that we have had another successful year. The Salamander Group has declared the largest profits in our history with sales breaking the two billion barrier. Last year we exported to 39 different countries and worldwide we employ nearly twenty-two thousand people.

As this is my last year I thought that I would say something about my time as chairperson of the group. I have enjoyed my time and in many ways it seems to have gone quickly even though I must say there were some very long days. During the last ten years there has been persistent and sometimes high inflation, fluctuating interest and exchange rates and levels of unemployment which we have not seen since before the Second World War. None of these factors have helped the United Kingdom's engineering industry. As a country we have to be able to compete on a world stage and our two main economic competitors Japan and West Germany have enjoyed more stable interest rates and exchange rates in recent times than we have. Inevitably this has helped them to be very competitive in certain sectors of the engineering market and it is one of the reasons why I decided that the company should diversify.

Diversification has meant that we are no longer dependent for our sales and profits on a single market and this has meant that we have been able to pay consistent dividends. I know that some of you may be thinking that they could have been bigger, but one thing I can assure you all is that we have reinvested our past profits wisely and these investments will yield the profits of the future.

I would like just to review the group's history since 1948 when Salamander Metal Industries, as the firm used to be called, first became a publicly quoted company on the London Stock Market. In those days all of our sales came from supplying marine engines. It's hard to believe it but in those days the British merchant navy still accounted for a large proportion of the world's tonnage. Sadly today this is no longer the case. Since 1979 our merchant fleet has been reduced from 30 million tons to 8 million and most new orders for ships go to foreign yards. This has made it harder for us to sell our marine engines, but I am pleased to say that we still have a strong association with the sea. Our interests now range from warehousing, ship chandlery, packing and freight forwarding, to house building, road haulage and waste disposal.

In my view it is this diversification which makes us strong. Not every one seems to realise this. The current bid from Tamar limited is not only unrealistic but will also see the end of our company. In their prospectus they have announced that they will keep our warehousing and haulage divisions and sell off everything else. Obviously they will make a handsome profit on the sale of our other companies because at present the stock market values our shares at slightly below our net assets. I believe that this is just a short term factor because the industrial sector has underperformed the rest of the market and fails to take account of our overall strength.

You will have seen our advertisements in the papers urging you to vote **no** to the Tamar bid. I am pleased to see that so many shareholders have come to the meeting today and I do urge you to think very carefully before you vote. Tamar have not yet been able to acquire a majority holding and I am hoping that our new chairperson Alison Towers will be able to steer the Salamander Group through these difficult times and that next year there will still be a shareholders meeting for the Salamander Group."

1 How can the Salamander Group's stock market capitalisation be less than its assets value?

2 Why is the Salamander Group vulnerable to a takeover?

3 What action can Alison Towers and her Board of Directors take to try and defeat the Tamar bid?

4 What factors should the Salamander Group's shareholders consider before deciding whether or not to accept the Tamar bid?

THE REN GROUP

The REN Group are considering investing 80,000 in new machinery. The firm is currently considering four new projects which they have called A,B,C and D. The costs and returns are shown below.

Initial Machine Investment

Project A	£50,000
Project B	£30,000
Project C	£20,000
Project D	£60,000

It has been estimated that at the end of five years each machine will have a residual value of 4% of its cost price. In addition the projects will require the following amounts of additional working capital, A £7,000, B £6,500, C £3,250 and D £8,150. The forecast returns are shown below.

Year	Project A £	B £	Forecast C £	Return D £
One	17,000	6,000	5,000	22,000
Two	24,000	9,000	8,000	40,000
Three	34,000	7,000	9,000	28,000
Four	27,000	5,400	7,000	16,000
Five	14,500	3,250	4,600	14,900

The directors are seeking a return on capital employed of 14%.

1 What factors should the firm consider before deciding which machines it should purchase with its capital budget of £80,000?

2 What are the limitations of investment appraisal techniques when considering new projects?

THE CHILTERN SAW MILL

During the last year there has been a big increase in the demand for wood in the United Kingdom. The Chiltern Saw Mill has been unable to capture as much of the market as it would have liked because it has lacked the industrial capacity. The Directors of the firm have agreed to borrow up to £90,000 from their bankers so that they can invest the money in their business. They are currently considering three projects which they have called A,B, and C.

The cash inflows over a six year period are shown below. All transactions are for cash and each project will have a residual value of nil. The cash flows are shown below. The Directors would like the project to earn a return of 10% but are currently facing working capital problems because of their rapid expansion programme.

		Projects		
		A	B	C
		£	£	£
Cash outflows	(Year 0)	90,000	72,000	63,000
Cash inflows	Year 1	20,000	25,000	15,000
	Year 2	34,000	33,000	30,000
	Year 3	42,000	39,000	35,000
	Year 4	57,000	45,000	39,000
	Year 5	46,000	47,000	38,500
	Year 6	38,000	42,000	35,000

The Directors would like you to calculate

1. the average net inflow

2. the annual depreciation

3. the average net profit

4. the average investment

5. the accounting rate of return

6. the pay back period in months

7. the net present value of each project

COPPER WARE LTD

Copper Ware Limited is a small firm in the West Midlands which manufactures copper kitchen products. Until recently all of its production was for the industrial catering market but it is now considering launching a range of copper based saucepans onto the consumer market.

The firm has developed three protype models. All are aimed at the more affluent consumer who is looking for a quality product to compliment their new cooker or kitchen. The costs of manufacturing and the company codes are given below.

	CSP109 £	CSP111 £	CSP120 £
Copper	6.00	5.00	4.00
Stainless Steel	7.00	5.00	3.00
Wooden Handle	2.00	2.00	2.00
Direct Labour	4.00	3.00	3.00
Variable Overhead	2.00	1.00	1.00
Selling Price	30.00	25.00	20.00

The firm's cost accountant has calculated that the fixed costs of production for a year will be £75,000 and that this cost should be equally apportioned among the three products.

1 Calculate the contribution which the firm will make on each saucepan sold?

2 What is the break-even point for each saucepan?

3 What are the dangers of apportioning fixed costs equally among the three products?

4 What are the limitations of break-even analysis?

2 What is the firm's break-even point for both products?

3 Assuming that the firm can only make one product, which one should it make?

THE SEASIDE RESTAURANT

The owners of the Seaside Restaurant are about to reopen their restaurant in time for the new season. Past experience has taught the management that their best selling products are hamburger and chips, breaded chicken and chips and sandwiches. Last year the firm sold the following products in the ratio of 4:2:1. The costs and selling price of the various meals are shown below.

	Hamburgers £	Chicken £	Sandwiches £
Selling Price	2.30	1.90	1.40
Cost of Food	0.80	0.90	0.40
Direct Labour	0.25	0 40	0.30
Variable Overhead	0.15	0.20	0.12
Time to Produce Each Meal in Minutes	10	15	6

The owners are currently purchasing the restaurant by means of a bank loan. The interest rate is fixed at 14% and the firm owe £60,000. In addition the owners have to pay other fixed costs of £7,000 per annum. There were no capital repayments during the year.

1 Calculate the contribution per meal sold?

2 What are the firm's fixed costs?

3 What is the firm's break even point for hamburgers, chicken and sandwiches?

4 If the firm can only sell one product which one should it sell?

5 Why is an understanding of the behaviour of costs important when setting prices?

MARKET REPORT

Market Report is a specialised weekly journal for people working in the financial services industry. Every week it carries articles on the current state of the world's stock markets and provides detailed analysis on the performance of unit trusts and other forms of investment. This week's headline read as follows;

INVESTORS STAY LIQUID AS BOND AND SHARE PRICES FALL.

This has been a bad week for world stock markets. Fears of higher interest rates world wide have caused shares and bond prices to be marked lower. In Tokyo the Nikei Index fell more than 200 points and in London the market was down by 60 points. By Friday afternoon New York was down 100 points but a late rally saw the index recover slightly to end the week 93 points down.

On Tuesday the Bundesbank raised its interest rates by 1% and once the London market received the news shares traded nervously. In America concern over the rising American trade defecit caused share prices to be marked lower and the falls continued on the Japanese stock markets. Fortunately the falls have not been as big as in October 1987 but market analysts are wondering what will happen during next week's trading. Much will depend on whether or not the major stock markets rally or enter a bearish phase. The only thing that is certain is that a bull market does not last forever but no one wishes to sell before it has reached its peak. Still that is the fun of the market and so investors will just have to wait a while before they know whether or not the bull market is over or whether it is about to enter its final phase. In the end it's all a matter of investor confidence.

1 Why do bond prices and share prices generally fall if interest rates rise?

2 What are share indexes and how is the Financial Times Share Index calculated?

3 What is meant by the terms a bull and a bear market?

4 What is meant by the term investor confidence and how does it affect share prices?

TYRE MASTER

Advertisement
Extracts From the Final Accounts

Your company goes from strength to strength as profits and sales increase in what must be called another record year.

Chairperson's statement shareholders' meeting 5 February 1990

	1989 £'000	1990 £'000
Turnover	12,540	14,320
Group profit before tax	2,197	2,458
Tax	350	362
Profit after tax	1,847	2,096
Minority Interests	212	242
Profit before Extraordinary Items	1,635	1,854
Extraordinary Items	135	210
Profit attributable to Tyre Master	1,770	2,064

Dividends

Preference	150	150
Ordinary	217	263
Retained Profit	1,403	1,786
Net Assets	7,100	8,350

1 Explain the following terms, Turnover, Minority Interests, Extraordinary Items, Preference Dividend, Ordinary Dividend, Retained Profit and Net Assets.

2 What is Tyre Master's capital?

3 What is Tyre Master's return on capital employed for the years 1989 and 1990?

4 Why do you think the firm has booked advertising space in newspapers to advertise its financial results?

DOORS UNLIMITED

Doors Unlimited is a small manufacturer of interior household doors. The firm has been trading for five years and has seen its profits and sales increase each year. The costs of production of its four best selling doors are shown below;

	A £	B £	C £	D £
Selling Price	40	36	20	60
Production Costs				
Direct Materials	15	11	9	25
Direct Labour	12	10	6	15
Variable Overhead	5	4	3	7
Sales in units	65,000	27,000	35,000	9,500

The Directors of Doors Unlimited has estimated that its fixed costs of manufacturing the four products are £225,000 and has apportioned the fixed costs among the four lines as follows. Product A 30%, B 25%, C 17% and the balance is apportioned to D.

The managing director knows that the firm is finding it hard to sell Product A and is considering withdrawing it from the market. He believes that by withdrawing Product A the overall profitability of the firm will improve.

You work for the company as a trainee accountant and have been asked to answer the following questions for the next Board of Directors meeting.

1 What is the marginal cost of producing Product A, B, C and D?

2 What is the break-even point for each product?

3 What is the profit or loss being made from the sale of each product?

4 Do you think that the Managing Director should withdraw Product A before launching a new product onto the market? Give your reasons?

MEJ BUILDERS

MEJ Builders are a small firm of builders. The company was started by three brothers who each gave their first initial to form the company name. They now specalise in motorway construction, have recently acquired new office premises and have recruited new staff to help them with the design and construction of a set of bridges over a newly-planned motorway. The actual building work is sub contracted so the firm is mainly concerned with the management of the project. Recently the company has been experiencing cash flow problems. As a result the directors are meeting their accountants to discuss their cash flow problems. You work as a trainee for the accountants and have been asked to prepare answers to the following questions.

MEJ Builder's Balance Sheet as at 31 January	1988 £	1989 £
Fixed Assets		
Office Premises	295.000	395,000
Fixtures & Fittings	30,000	50,000
Motor Vehicles	15,000	30,000
	340,000	475,000
Current Assets		
Stock	20,000	85,000
Debtors	15,000	45,000
Bank	5,000	-

Current Liabilities

Creditors	10,000	25,000
Bank Overdraft	-	45.000
Net Assets	370,000	535,000

Capital

Share Capital	150,000	250,000
Profit & Loss A/C	20,000	85,000
Bank Loan	150,000	150,000
German Currency Loan	50,000	50,000
	370,000	535,000

1 What is meant by the term working capital?

2 What steps should MEJ Builders take to conserve their working capital?

3 Prepare a statement showing changes in the firm's working capital during the past year and prepare a report to explain your findings.

GLOSSARY

Accelerator
Change in net investment / change in consumption.

Autonomous Investment
Investment which is independant of the level of income, output and the general level of economic activity.

Balance Sheet
Statement of a firm's assets and liabilities.

Balance of Payments
A statement showing the relationship between total payments into and out of a country in a given period, usually one year.

Balance of Trade
The net result of payments made and received in connection with the purchase and sale of tangible goods (visibles).

Black Economy
Illegal economic activity which avoids paying tax, particularly VAT and Income Tax.

Break-Even
The point where total revenue equals total cost.

Business Cycle
Changes in the level of business activity from boom to recession to slump to recovery and boom again.

Capital
A factor of production in the form of a stock of producers' goods which are available for use in production.

Accountants use the term to describe the amount of money which is financing a firm.

Capital Expenditure
Money spent on fixed assets, i.e. those held in the business long-term.

Capital Loss
Loss made on the sale of a fixed asset.

Centralisation
The concentration of authority in the hands of a few people at the head of an organisation.

Contribution
The difference between sales revenue and the variable cost of those sales.

Cyclical Unemployment
Sometimes called demand deficiency unemployment. It occurs when total spending in the economy falls, so that the general demand for goods and services falls.

Debenture
Normally a secured loan over the fixed assets of a company.

Decentralisation
Where decision-making is delegated to the lowest practicable levels in a firm.

Diseconomies of Scale
Problems of firms becoming larger e.g. difficult to control.

Dissaving
This occurs when people spend more on consumption than they are earning from income by either reducing their savings or borrowing more.

Diversification
Spreading business operations over different products and/or areas in order to reduce risks of failure.

Division of Labour
Dividing work into specialised occupations/tasks.

Economic Growth
Increased productive capacity, leading to increased national income per head over time.

Economies of Scale
Benefits of firms growing larger, e.g. lower unit costs, because their bulk purchasing power enables them to buy raw materials at lower prices.

Exchange Rate
The price of one currency in terms of another e.g. £1 = $1.70.

Frictional Unemployment
Temporary unemployment between leaving one job and finding another

Gross National Expenditure
The total value of all goods and services in monetary terms spent by households, foreigners (by purchasing exports), business and government on a nation's output of goods and services.

Horizontal Combination
Integration of firms at the same stage of production e.g. two manufacturing firms.

Industrial Concentration
Where certain (or most) industries are concentrated into certain areas.

In-house Training
Any training of workers which takes place within the organisation in which they work.

Marginal Cost
The cost of producing one extra unit of output.

In accounting the term is used to describe the variable cost of producing a good or service.

Market Economy
An economic system where people are free to buy whatever they think they need and can afford, and in which producers supply whatever they think they can sell at a profit.

Marketing
Management process responsible for identifying, anticipating and satisfying customer requirements profitably. (Chartered Institute of Marketing)

Mixed Economy
An economy where some factors of production are owned by the state while others are owned by private individuals and firms.

Monopoly
Market where a firm produces a good or service and where there are no close substitutes.

Multinational Company
A large company with factories/selling agencies in several countries.

Multiplier
Change in income/Change in Investment.

Nominal Value
The face value of a share, as distinct from its market price.

Objectives
Business goals stated in specific terms, e.g. to increase sales by 10%, before the end of one year and without increasing expenditure by more than 5%.

Planned Economy
Also called a collective or command economy; where land and capital are owned by state and workers are allocated to jobs.

Policy
A strategy or plan of action in order to achieve objectives.

Primary Industries
Extractive industries like mining, querrying and farming.

Prime Cost
The total variable or direct costs of production.

Regional Policy
Government measures to reduce regional imbalance in a country e.g. assisting deprived areas.

Reserve
Company profits kept in the business for future use. (Governments also hold reserves of gold/currency).

Secondary Industries
Manufacturing, construction and similar insdustries which use the raw materials provided by primary industry.

Share Premium
When a company's shares are sold above nominal value, the surplus is the share premium.

Subsidy
Financial assistance, usually in the form of a government grant.

Takeover
Where one business buys out and takes control of another.

Tertiary Industries
Service industries like transport, retailing, communications.

Vertical Combination
Integration of firms at successive stages of production, e.g. mining company with a manufactoring company using its raw materials.

Working Capital
Current assets less current liabilities.

DCF TABLES

Compound Sum of £1 (CVIF) $S = P(1 + r)^N$

Period	1%	2%	3%	4%	5%	6%	7%
1	1.010	1.020	1.030	1.040	1.050	1.060	1.070
2	1.020	1.040	1.061	1.082	1.102	1.124	1.145
3	1.030	1.061	1.093	1.125	1.158	1.191	1.225
4	1.041	1.082	1.126	1.170	1.216	1.262	1.311
5	1.051	1.104	1.159	1.217	1.276	1.338	1.403
6	1.062	1.126	1.194	1.265	1.340	1.419	1.501
7	1.072	1.149	1.230	1.316	1.407	1.504	1.606
8	1.083	1.172	1.267	1.369	1.477	1.594	1.718
9	1.094	1.195	1.305	1.423	1.551	1.689	1.838
10	1.105	1.219	1.344	1.480	1.629	1.791	1.967
11	1.116	1.243	1.384	1.539	1.710	1.898	2.105
12	1.127	1.268	1.426	1.601	1.796	2.012	2.252
13	1.138	1.294	1.469	1.665	1.886	2.133	2.410
14	1.149	1.319	1.513	1.732	1.980	2.261	2.579
15	1.161	1.346	1.558	1.801	2.079	2.397	2.759
16	1.173	1.373	1.605	1.873	2.183	2.540	2.952
17	1.184	1.400	1.653	1.948	2.292	2.693	3.159
18	1.196	1.428	1.702	2.026	2.407	2.854	3.380
19	1.208	1.457	1.754	2.107	2.527	3.026	3.617
20	1.220	1.486	1.806	2.191	2.653	3.207	3.870
25	1.282	1.641	2.094	2.666	3.386	4.292	5.427
30	1.348	1.811	2.427	3.243	4.322	5.743	7.612

Period	8%	9%	10%	12%	14%	15%	16%
1	1.080	1.090	1.100	1.120	1.140	1.150	1.160
2	1.166	1.186	1.210	1.254	1.300	1.322	1.346
3	1.260	1.295	1.331	1.405	1.482	1.521	1.561
4	1.360	1.412	1.464	1.574	1.689	1.749	1.811
5	1.469	1.539	1.611	1.762	1.925	2.011	2.100
6	1.587	1.677	1.772	1.974	2.195	2.313	2.436
7	1.714	1.828	1.949	2.211	2.502	2.660	2.826
8	1.851	1.993	2.144	2.476	2.853	3.059	3.278
9	1.999	2.172	2.358	2.773	3.252	3.518	3.803
10	2.159	2.367	2.594	3.106	3.707	4.046	4.411
11	2.332	2.580	2.853	3.479	4.226	4.652	5.117
12	2.518	2.813	3.138	3.896	4.818	5.350	5.926
13	2.720	3.066	3.452	4.363	5.492	6.153	6.886
14	2.937	3.342	3.797	4.887	6.261	7.076	7.988
15	3.172	3.642	4.177	5.474	7.138	8.137	9.266
16	3.426	3.970	4.595	6.130	8.137	9.358	10.748
17	3.700	4.328	5.054	6.866	9.276	10.761	12.468
18	3.996	4.717	5.560	7.690	10.575	12.375	14.463
19	4.316	5.142	6.116	8.613	12.056	14.232	16.777
20	4.661	5.604	6.728	9.646	13.743	16.367	19.461
25	6.848	8.623	10.835	17.000	26.462	32.919	40.874
30	10.063	13.268	17.449	29.960	50.950	66.212	85.850

Present Value of £1 (PVIF) $P = S(1+r)^{-N}$

Period	1%	2%	3%	4%	5%	6%	7%	8%	9%	10%	12%	14%	15%
1	0.990	0.980	0.971	0.962	0.952	0.943	0.935	0.926	0.917	0.909	0.893	0.877	0.870
2	0.980	0.961	0.943	0.925	0.907	0.890	0.873	0.857	0.842	0.826	0.797	0.769	0.756
3	0.971	0.942	0.915	0.889	0.864	0.840	0.816	0.794	0.772	0.751	0.712	0.675	0.658
4	0.961	0.924	0.889	0.855	0.823	0.792	0.763	0.735	0.708	0.683	0.636	0.592	0.572
5	0.951	0.906	0.863	0.822	0.784	0.747	0.713	0.681	0.650	0.621	0.567	0.519	0.497
6	0.942	0.888	0.838	0.790	0.746	0.705	0.666	0.630	0.596	0.564	0.507	0.456	0.432
7	0.933	0.871	0.813	0.760	0.711	0.665	0.623	0.583	0.547	0.513	0.452	0.400	0.376
8	0.923	0.853	0.789	0.731	0.677	0.627	0.582	0.540	0.502	0.467	0.404	0.351	0.327
9	0.914	0.837	0.766	0.703	0.645	0.592	0.544	0.500	0.460	0.424	0.361	0.308	0.284
10	0.905	0.820	0.744	0.676	0.614	0.558	0.508	0.463	0.422	0.386	0.322	0.270	0.247
11	0.896	0.804	0.722	0.650	0.585	0.527	0.475	0.429	0.388	0.350	0.287	0.237	0.215
12	0.887	0.788	0.701	0.625	0.557	0.497	0.444	0.397	0.356	0.319	0.257	0.208	0.187
13	0.879	0.773	0.681	0.601	0.530	0.469	0.415	0.368	0.326	0.290	0.229	0.182	0.163
14	0.870	0.758	0.661	0.577	0.505	0.442	0.388	0.340	0.299	0.263	0.205	0.160	0.141
15	0.861	0.743	0.642	0.555	0.481	0.417	0.362	0.315	0.275	0.239	0.183	0.140	0.123
16	0.853	0.728	0.623	0.534	0.458	0.394	0.339	0.292	0.252	0.218	0.163	0.123	0.107
17	0.844	0.714	0.605	0.513	0.436	0.371	0.317	0.270	0.231	0.198	0.146	0.108	0.093
18	0.836	0.700	0.587	0.494	0.416	0.350	0.296	0.250	0.212	0.180	0.130	0.095	0.081
19	0.828	0.686	0.570	0.475	0.396	0.331	0.276	0.232	0.194	0.164	0.116	0.083	0.070
20	0.820	0.673	0.554	0.456	0.377	0.312	0.258	0.215	0.178	0.149	0.104	0.073	0.061
25	0.780	0.610	0.478	0.375	0.295	0.233	0.184	0.146	0.116	0.092	0.059	0.038	0.030
30	0.742	0.552	0.412	0.308	0.231	0.174	0.131	0.099	0.075	0.057	0.033	0.020	0.015

Present Value of £1 (PVIF) $P = S(1 + r)^{-N}$ cont.

Period	16%	18%	20%	24%	28%	32%	36%	40%	50%	60%	70%	80%	90%
1	0.862	0.847	0.833	0.806	0.781	0.758	0.735	0.714	0.667	0.625	0.588	0.556	0.526
2	0.743	0.718	0.694	0.650	0.610	0.574	0.541	0.510	0.444	0.391	0.346	0.309	0.277
3	0.641	0.609	0.579	0.524	0.477	0.435	0.398	0.364	0.296	0.244	0.204	0.171	0.146
4	0.552	0.516	0.482	0.423	0.373	0.329	0.292	0.260	0.198	0.153	0.120	0.095	0.077
5	0.476	0.437	0.402	0.341	0.291	0.250	0.215	0.186	0.132	0.095	0.070	0.053	0.040
6	0.410	0.370	0.335	0.275	0.227	0.189	0.158	0.133	0.088	0.060	0.041	0.029	0.021
7	0.354	0.314	0.279	0.222	0.178	0.143	0.116	0.095	0.059	0.037	0.024	0.016	0.011
8	0.305	0.266	0.233	0.179	0.139	0.108	0.085	0.068	0.039	0.023	0.014	0.009	0.006
9	0.263	0.226	0.194	0.144	0.108	0.082	0.063	0.048	0.026	0.015	0.008	0.005	0.003
10	0.227	0.191	0.162	0.116	0.085	0.062	0.046	0.035	0.017	0.009	0.005	0.003	0.002
11	0.195	0.162	0.135	0.094	0.066	0.047	0.034	0.025	0.012	0.006	0.003	0.002	0.001
12	0.168	0.137	0.112	0.076	0.052	0.036	0.025	0.018	0.008	0.004	0.002	0.001	0.001
13	0.145	0.116	0.093	0.061	0.040	0.027	0.018	0.013	0.005	0.002	0.001	0.001	0.000
14	0.125	0.099	0.078	0.049	0.032	0.021	0.014	0.009	0.003	0.001	0.001	0.000	0.000
15	0.108	0.084	0.065	0.040	0.025	0.016	0.010	0.006	0.002	0.001	0.000	0.000	0.000
16	0.093	0.071	0.054	0.032	0.019	0.012	0.007	0.005	0.002	0.001	0.000	0.000	
17	0.080	0.060	0.045	0.026	0.015	0.009	0.005	0.003	0.001	0.000	0.000		
18	0.089	0.051	0.038	0.021	0.012	0.007	0.004	0.002	0.001	0.000	0.000		
19	0.060	0.043	0.031	0.017	0.009	0.005	0.003	0.002	0.000	0.000	0.000		
20	0.051	0.037	0.026	0.014	0.007	0.004	0.002	0.001	0.000	0.000	0.000		
25	0.024	0.016	0.010	0.005	0.002	0.001	0.000	0.000					
30	0.012	0.007	0.004	0.002	0.001	0.000	0.000	0.000					

A Manager's Guide to Quantitative Methods

Michael Cuming

isbn 0 946139 01 6   £8.90   Paperback

An unusual and comprehensive introduction to
quantitative methods using topical examples
and diagrams to analyse real problems
and suggest solutions.

A user-friendly book for managers who need
to appreciate the uses, misuses and potentialities
of quantitative methods.

CONTENTS

Frequency distributions
Getting the right answer from your calculator
Summarising distributions
The language of uncertainty
Simplifying data
Compound interest and discounting
Correlation and regression
Tracking things in time
Finding out by sampling
Drawing conclusions
Managing with the computer
Problems with data

'Overall this book is a comprehensive guide to quantitative
methods and *truly should require no previous mathematical
knowledge...* It is worth serious consideration for
a wide range of management courses.
V.J. Seddon in *Natfhe Journal* February, 1985.

TRAVEL & TOURISM

Second Edition

Patrick Lavery

A detailed introduction to the study of tourism for courses
at BTEC HND level and the first year of a degree.

Full coverage of the main sectors of the tourism industry;
based on extensive research by the author. Now updated,
extended and with new material for the second edition.

Defines the tourism industry and outlines its development in
Britain, Europe and the United States. It includes transport
deregulation, Tourism Development Action Plans and
innovation in Tourism Development in Britain & Europe.

CONTENTS

The tourism industry/its development and structure
International tourism: an overview
The retail travel sector
The passenger transport sector
The accommodation sector
Public sector tourism
Planning & development of tourism
Tourism marketing
Tourism impact studies: economic/environmental
New developments in tourism

Illustrations, maps, tables & comprehensive index

Sewn paperback £7.50 isbn 1 85450 120 8

TUTOR'S PACK

Second edition of the popular set of tested exercises with
notes, model answers and other materials
(including overhead projection transparencies)
to support and extend the textbook.

Presentation looseleaf binder isbn 1 85450 130 5
£39.00 (gratis with 15 copies of the book bought direct)

CASE STUDIES IN MANAGEMENT

private sector, introductory level

second edition

edited by Sheila Ritchie

A topical and interesting collection of real-life business
case studies based on mainly small and medium-sized
companies. There are nine mini-cases (short incident
studies) and ten longer, cross-functional cases.
There is an interesting mix of products and services, from
chemicals and valves to books and leisure.

Sewn paperback   £7.95   isbn 0 946139 02 4

TUTOR'S PACK

The Tutor's Pack comprises model answers, notes and
other materials (including some computer programs and 6
overhead projector transparencies). All cases in the book
have been tested on business management students and
the notes in the Tutor's Pack build on that experience.

Bound in a presentation file with loose insert plastic pockets
£49.00 (gratis with 15 copies of the book bought direct)

isbn 0 946139 07 5

MRS THATCHER'S CASEBOOK

Non-partisan studies in Conservative Government policy

Terry Garrison

Well-researched case studies of ten major crises handled
by Mrs Thatcher's government.

Inner city time bomb ?
The Falklands War
GCHQ
Deregulation of the buses
London Transport - Fares Fair
The coal strike
Flexible rostering - British Rail
British Steel
The De Lorean dream
British Leyland

Includes a large section on policy analysis for managers.

Hardback binding   £19.95 (student edition/bulk £9.95)
isbn 0 946139 86 5

TUTOR'S PACK

Case notes, chronologies, commentary and other material
to supplement, support and extend the text.

Presentation looseleaf binder   £59.00 (gratis with 15 books)
isbn 0 946139 46 6

EMPLOYEE RELATIONS

an introduction

Ken Whitehead

Employee Relations describes the system by which employers
and Trade Unions seek to resolve their differences,
and reveals that disputes are not entirely concerned
with a particular workplace or set of rules.
Rather problems at work are a focal point of wider
issues arising from the very nature of industrial society.

CONTENTS

Why Trade Unions ?
Why so many Trade Unions ?
How are Trade Unions governed ?
What is an Employers' Association ?
The TUC and the CBI
International organisation
The role of management
The role of shop stewards
The organisation of bargaining
The practice of collective bargaining
The role of State and Government
Industrial democracy and participation
Pressures on the present system
Getting it together again

Book -   isbn 0 946139 76 8   £8.95

Tutor's Pack of tested exercises, notes, overhead projection
transparencies and other materials to support and extend
the textbook - isbn 0 946139 81 4   £39.00

WORK FOR WORK

A workbook for the mature job seeker

Michael Weatherley & Michael Ryan

Designed to help managers, professionals and other mature
people to find work. Starting with self-analysis, it
takes readers through the complex process of looking for a new
job, career or business opportunity, giving sound, practical
on organising and mounting a successful search.

It is a workbook, not a textbook. Tasks are set at each stage
so that individuals can develop and test their expectations,
perceptions and skills; analyse the market; evaluate their
own campaigns; and find appropriate, satisfying work.

Work for Work is based on successful courses for the mature
unemployed. It has been helpful to those wishing to
change career or to make an effective transition into
work which is new and rewarding.

Some of the topics covered:

the database
managing your career
decision making
alternatives to employment
the interview
offers/no offers
starting work

Wire bound (for ease of use)   £6.95   isbn 0 946139 51 2

PERSONNEL MANAGEMENT IN CONTEXT
the late 1980s

Terry McIlwee

A set book at many colleges for the IPM Stage 1 paper - it is a 'valuable text for personnel specialists as well as students', bringing together 'a large amount of relevant research in a concise, readable review.' (Jane Granatt in Industrial Society).

'The book succeeds in its main aim... the section on legislation is particularly well laid out & should prove handy in many personnel departments where a quick reminder...is often required.' (John Foulds in Personnel Management).

isbn 0 946139 35 0   £10.90 paperback 352 pp. Winter 1986

TOURISM LAW

Jim Corke

The first text specially written on the law relating to travel & tourism. Designed for people who are not law specialists, and for students of hospitality, travel, recreation & leisure on courses from BTEC to degree level.

isbn 0 946139 95 4   £10.95   Winter 1988

Tutor's Manual

With formal assignments, set work for skills development and role play; supported by contemporary documentary evidence.

Looseleaf A4 binder   isbn 0 946139 96 2   £39.00